T0183156

Lecture Notes in Computer Science 14206

Founding Editors

Gerhard Goos
Juris Hartmanis

Editorial Board Members

The series Lecture Notes in Computer Science (LNCS), including its subseries Lecture Notes in Artificial Intelligence (LNAI) and Lecture Notes in Bioinformatics (LNBI), has established itself as a medium for the publication of new developments in computer science and information technology research, teaching, and education.

LNCS enjoys close cooperation with the computer science R & D community, the series counts many renowned academics among its volume editors and paper authors, and collaborates with prestigious societies. Its mission is to serve this international community by providing an invaluable service, mainly focused on the publication of conference and workshop proceedings and postproceedings. LNCS commenced publication in 1973.

Qin Wang · Jun Feng · Liang-Jie Zhang
Editors

Blockchain – ICBC 2023

6th International Conference
Held as Part of the Services Conference Federation, SCF 2023
Honolulu, HI, USA, September 23–26, 2023
Proceedings

 Springer

Editors
Qin Wang
CSIRO Data61
Eveleigh, NSW, Australia

Jun Feng
Huazhong University of Science
and Technology
Wuhan, China

Liang-Jie Zhang (iD)
Shenzhen Entrepreneurship and Innovation
Federation (SEIF)
Shenzhen, China

ISSN 0302-9743   ISSN 1611-3349 (electronic)
Lecture Notes in Computer Science
ISBN 978-3-031-44919-2   ISBN 978-3-031-44920-8 (eBook)
https://doi.org/10.1007/978-3-031-44920-8

This Springer imprint is published by the registered company Springer Nature Switzerland AG
The registered company address is: Gewerbestrasse 11, 6330 Cham, Switzerland

Paper in this product is recyclable.

Preface

The International Conference on Blockchain (ICBC) aims to provide an international forum for both researchers and industry practitioners to exchange the latest fundamental advances in the state-of-the-art technologies and best practices of blockchain, as well as emerging standards and research topics which will define the future of blockchain.

This volume presents the accepted papers for the International Conference on Blockchain (ICBC 2023), held as a hybrid conference during September 23–26, 2023 On-Site in Honolulu, Hawaii, USA, with Satellite Sessions in Shenzhen, Guangdong, China and also Online for those unable to attend on-site. All topics regarding blockchain technologies, platforms, solutions, and business models were aligned with the theme of ICBC. Topics of interest included, but were not limited to, new blockchain architectures, platform constructions, blockchain development, and blockchain services technologies as well as standards and the blockchain services innovation lifecycle, including enterprise modeling, business consulting, solution creation, services orchestration, services optimization, services management, services marketing, and business process integration and management.

We accepted 9 full papers and no short papers, from 18 submissions. Each was reviewed and selected by at least three independent members of the ICBC 2023 International Program Committee in a single-blind review process. We are pleased to thank the authors whose submissions and participation made this conference possible. We also want to express our thanks to the Program Committee members for their dedication in helping to organize the conference and reviewing the submissions.

August 2023

Qin Wang
Jun Feng
Liang-Jie Zhang

Organization

General Chair

Shiping Chen   CSIRO Data61 & UNSW, Australia

Program Chairs

Qin Wang   CSIRO Data61, Australia
Jun Feng   Huazhong University of Science and Technology, China

Services Conference Federation (SCF 2023)

General Chairs

Ali Arsanjani   Google, USA
Wu Chou   Essenlix Corporation, USA

Program Chair

Liang-Jie Zhang   Shenzhen Entrepreneurship and Innovation Federation, China

CFO

Min Luo   Georgia Tech, USA

Operation Committee

Jing Zeng   China Gridcom Co., Ltd., China
Yishuang Ning   Tsinghua University, China
Sheng He   Tsinghua University, China

Steering Committee

Calton Pu (Co-chair)	Georgia Tech, USA
Liang-Jie Zhang (Co-Chair)	Shenzhen Entrepreneurship and Innovation Federation, China

ICBC 2023 Program Committee

Adel Elmessiry	ALPHAFIN, USA
Xinxin Fan	IoTeX, USA
Chao Li	Beijing Jiaotong University, China
Catalin Meirosu	Ericsson, Sweden
Lei Xu	Kent State University, USA
Rui Zhang	Institute of Information Engineering, Chinese Academy of Sciences, China
Arnab Chatterjee	R3, India
Roberto Di Pietro	King Abdullah University of Science and Technology, Saudi Arabia
Rudrapatna Shyamasundar	Indian Institute of Technology Bombay, India
Andreas Veneris	University of Toronto, Canada

Conference Sponsor – Services Society

The Services Society (S2) is a non-profit professional organization that has been created to promote worldwide research and technical collaboration in services innovations among academia and industrial professionals. Its members are volunteers from industry and academia with common interests. S2 is registered in the USA as a "501(c) organization", which means that it is an American tax-exempt nonprofit organization. S2 collaborates with other professional organizations to sponsor or co-sponsor conferences and to promote an effective services curriculum in colleges and universities. S2 initiates and promotes a "Services University" program worldwide to bridge the gap between industrial needs and university instruction.

The Services Sector has account for 79.5% of the GDP of United States in 2016. In fact, Hong Kong accounts for 90%. The Services Society has formed 5 Special Interest Groups (5 SIGs) to support technology- and domain-specific...

- Special Interest Group on Services Computing (SIG-SC)
- Special Interest Group on Big Data (SIG-BD)
- Special Interest Group on Cloud Computing (SIG-CLOUD)
- Special Interest Group on Artificial Intelligence (SIG-AI)
- Special Interest Group on Metaverse (SIG-Metaverse)

About the Services Conference Federation (SCF)

As the founding member of the Services Conference Federation (SCF), the first International Conference on Web Services (ICWS) was held in June 2003 in Las Vegas, USA. Meanwhile, the First International Conference on Web Services - Europe 2003 (ICWS-Europe 2003) was held in Germany in October 2003. ICWS-Europe 2003 was an extended event of the 2003 International Conference on Web Services (ICWS 2003) in Europe. In 2004, ICWS-Europe was changed to the European Conference on Web Services (ECOWS), which was held at Erfurt, Germany.

2023 Services Conference Federation (SCF 2023, www.icws.org) was a hybrid conference On-Site in Honolulu, Hawaii, USA, with Satellite Sessions in Shenzhen, Guangdong, China and also Online for those could not attend on-site. All the virtual conference presentations were given via pre-recorded videos during September 23–26, 2023 through the BigMarker Video Broadcasting Platform: https://www.bigmarker.com/series/services-conference-federati/series_summit.

To present a new form and improve the impact of the conference, we also planned an Automatic Webinar which was presented by experts in various fields. All the invited talks were given via pre-recorded videos and broadcast in a live-like form recursively by two session channels during the conference period. Each invited talk was converted into an on-demand webinar right after the conference.

In the past 20 years, the ICWS community has expanded from Web engineering innovations to scientific research for the whole services industry. Service delivery platforms have been expanded to mobile platforms, Internet of Things, cloud computing, and edge computing. The services ecosystem has gradually been enabled, value added, and intelligence embedded through enabling technologies such as big data, artificial intelligence, and cognitive computing. In the coming years, all transactions with multiple parties involved will be transformed to blockchain.

Based on technology trends and best practices in the field, the Services Conference Federation (SCF) will continue serving as the conference umbrella's code name for all services-related conferences. SCF 2023 defined the future of New ABCDE (AI, Blockchain, Cloud, BigData & IOT). We are very proud to announce that SCF 2023's 10 co-located theme topic conferences all centered around "services", with each focusing on exploring different themes (web-based services, cloud-based services, Big Data-based services, services innovation lifecycle, AI-driven ubiquitous services, blockchain driven trust service-ecosystems, Metaverse services and applications, and emerging service-oriented technologies).

Some highlights of SCF 2023 are shown below:

– **Bigger Platform**: The 10 collocated conferences (SCF 2023) were sponsored by the Services Society, which is the world-leading not-for-profit organization (501 c(3)) dedicated to the service of more than 30,000 worldwide Services Computing researchers and practitioners. A bigger platform means bigger opportunities for all volunteers, authors and participants. Meanwhile, Springer provided sponsorship to best paper awards and other professional activities. All the 10 conference proceedings of SCF 2023 were published by Springer and indexed in ISI Conference Proceedings Citation Index (included in Web of Science), Engineering Index EI (Compendex and Inspec databases), DBLP, Google Scholar, IO-Port, MathSciNet, Scopus, and ZBlMath.

- **Brighter Future**: While celebrating 2023 version of ICWS, SCF 2023 highlighted the International Conference on Blockchain (ICBC 2023) and the International Conference on Metaverse (Metaverse 2023) to build the fundamental infrastructure for enabling secure and trusted services ecosystems. This will lead our community members to create their own brighter future.
- **Better Model**: SCF 2023 continued to leverage the invented Conference Blockchain Model (CBM) to innovate the organizing practices for all the 10 theme conferences. Senior researchers in the field are welcome to submit proposals to serve as CBM Ambassador for an individual conference to start better interactions during your leadership role in organizing future SCF conferences.

Member of SCF 2023

The Services Conference Federation (SCF) includes 10 service-oriented conferences: ICWS, CLOUD, SCC, BigData Congress, AIMS, METAVERSE, ICIOT, EDGE, ICCC and ICBC.

[1] 2023 International Conference on Web Services (ICWS 2023, http://icws.org/2023) was the flagship theme-topic conference for Web-centric services, enabling technologies and applications.

[2] 2023 International Conference on Cloud Computing (CLOUD 2023, http://thecloudcomputing.org/2023) was the flagship theme-topic conference for resource sharing, utility-like usage models, IaaS, PaaS, and SaaS.

[3] 2023 International Conference on Big Data (BigData 2023, http://bigdatacongress.org/2023) was the theme-topic conference for data sourcing, data processing, data analysis, data-driven decision making, and data-centric applications.

[4] 2023 International Conference on Services Computing (SCC 2023, http://thescc.org/2023) was the flagship theme-topic conference for leveraging the latest computing technologies to design, develop, deploy, operate, manage, modernize, and redesign business services.

[5] 2023 International Conference on AI & Mobile Services (AIMS 2023, http://ai1000.org/2023) was the theme-topic conference for artificial intelligence, neural networks, machine learning, training data sets, AI scenarios, AI delivery channels, and AI supporting infrastructure as well as mobile internet services. The goal of AIMS was to bring AI to any mobile devices and other channels.

[6] 2023 International Conference on Metaverse (Metaverse 2023, http://metaverse1000.org/2023) put its focus on all innovations of the Metaverse industry, including financial services, education services, transportation services, energy services, government services, manufacturing services, consulting services, and other industry services.

[7] 2023 International Conference on Cognitive Computing (ICCC 2023, http://thecog nitivecomputing.org/2023) put its focus on leveraging the latest computing technologies to simulate, model, implement, and realize cognitive sensing and brain operating systems.

[8] 2023 International Conference on Internet of Things (ICIOT 2023, http://iciot.org/2023) put its focus on the science, technology, and applications of IOT device innovations as well as IOT services in various solution scenarios.

[9] 2023 International Conference on Edge Computing (EDGE 2023, http://theedgeco mputing.org/2023) was a theme-topic conference for leveraging the latest computing technologies to enable localized device connections, edge gateways, edge applications, edge-cloud interactions, edge-user experiences, and edge business models.

[10] 2023 International Conference on Blockchain (ICBC 2023, http://blockchain1000. org/2023) concentrated on all aspects of blockchain, including digital currency, distributed application development, industry-specific blockchains, public blockchains, community blockchains, private blockchains, blockchain-based services, and enabling technologies.

Contents

Research Track

DARSAN: A Decentralized Review System Suitable for NFT Marketplaces

Sulyab Thottungal Valapu[1]($\boxtimes$), Tamoghna Sarkar[1], Jared Coleman[1],
Anusha Avyukt[1], Hugo Embrechts[2], Dimitri Torfs[2], Michele Minelli[2],
and Bhaskar Krishnamachari[1]

[1] University of Southern California, Los Angeles, USA
{thottung,tsarkar,jaredcol,aavyukt,bkrishna}@usc.edu
[2] SONY R and D Center Brussels Laboratory, Brussels, Belgium
{hugo.embrechts,dimitri.torfs,michele.minelli}@sony.com

Abstract. We introduce DARSAN, a decentralized review system designed for Non-Fungible Token (NFT) marketplaces, to address the challenge of verifying the quality of highly resalable products with few verified buyers by incentivizing unbiased reviews. DARSAN works by iteratively selecting a group of reviewers (called "experts") who are likely to both accurately predict the objective popularity and assess some subjective quality of the assets uniquely associated with NFTs. The system consists of a two-phased review process: a "pre-listing" phase where only experts can review the product, and a "pre-sale" phase where any reviewer on the system can review the product. Upon completion of the sale, DARSAN distributes incentives to the participants and selects the next generation of experts based on the performance of both experts and non-expert reviewers. We evaluate DARSAN through simulation and show that, once bootstrapped with an initial set of appropriately chosen experts, DARSAN favors honest reviewers and improves the quality of the expert pool over time without any external intervention even in the presence of potentially malicious participants.

Keywords: NFT · marketplace · review system · blockchain

1 Introduction

Ratings and reviews have a significant impact on the perception of potential customers regarding the quality of a product [9,21]. Therefore, it is in the interest of online marketplaces to promote helpful and high-quality reviews, while demoting biased or low-value ones. Although challenging for any online marketplace [3], designing a review system for Non-Fungible Token (NFT) marketplaces presents unique difficulties due to their scarcity and high resale potential. The sale of an NFT collection, typically limited to a few hundred or thousand pieces, creates two groups of users: a minority who own one of the NFTs and a supermajority who do not. The high resale potential of NFTs creates an incentive for the minority to rate them highly, irrespective of their true opinion, in the hopes of reselling them at a higher price in the future. Conversely, the non-owning super-majority have less incentive to rate the NFTs positively and may even rate them poorly to decrease their value, thereby increasing their chances of obtaining the NFTs for a lower price in the future, or to increase the relative value of the NFTs they own. As of February 2023, none of the top five NFT marketplaces ranked by trading volume (Blur, OpenSea, X2Y2, Magic Eden, LooksRare) [14] have integrated rating or review systems, which further supports this argument. Instead, these marketplaces rely on indirect metrics such as the number of users who viewed or "favorited" an NFT, which can be easily gamed.

In this paper, we introduce DARSAN, a decentralized review system designed for Non-Fungible Token (NFT) marketplaces that aims to address this issue. DARSAN utilizes an approach where a group of reviewers, known as "experts" are iteratively selected based on their ability to accurately predict the objective popularity and assess some subjective quality of the assets uniquely associated with NFTs. While the objective popularity is measured using ground truths associated with sales, such as sale price or volume, DARSAN does not require the system to explicitly define *any* rubric to assess the subjective quality of an asset. Instead, it relies on expert consensus to implicitly establish the rubric at any given time. The review process consists of two phases: a "pre-listing" phase, where only experts can review the product, and a "pre-sale" phase, where any reviewer on the system can review the product. After the sale, DARSAN distributes economic as well as non-economic incentives to the participants and selects the next generation of experts based on the performance of both expert and non-expert reviewers. Figure 1 illustrates the interaction between DARSAN and an NFT marketplace.

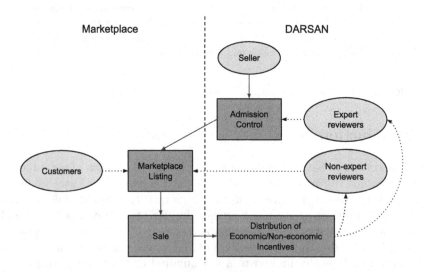

Fig. 1. Illustration of the integration of DARSAN within an NFT marketplace. The red ovals symbolize different roles, i.e., an individual may simultaneously act as a customer and a reviewer. (Color figure online)

DARSAN has numerous features that make it an attractive option to marketplace owners and users alike. One of its most significant advantages is *versatility*, as it enables marketplace owners to achieve a balance between the relative significance of subjective opinions (e.g., expert reviews) and objective data (e.g., sales metrics) by choosing system parameters appropriately. Once deployed, DARSAN is *self-sufficient*, requiring no further involvement from the marketplace owner. Furthermore, DARSAN ensures *transparency* through blockchain logging, which allows for all actions to be publicly verifiable. This eliminates the possibility of manipulative practices by marketplace owners, such as "shadow banning" and falsification of product ratings, which have been increasingly reported in recent years [11,13,16].

We performed numerical simulations to assess the effectiveness of DARSAN in identifying new generations of experts and its resistance to adversarial behavior from expert as well as non-expert participants. Our findings suggest that once the system is bootstrapped with an initial set of "appropriately" chosen experts, DARSAN incentivizes honest reviewers, leading to an improvement in the quality of the expert pool over time, even in the presence of potentially malicious participants. The system accomplishes this without any external intervention, which makes it an ideal option for a decentralized review system for highly resalable products that have few verified buyers, such as NFT marketplaces and art markets. Moreover, the ability of the system to combine subjective opinions and objective metrics for decentralized decision-making makes it ideal for integration into other decentralized systems.

2   Related Work

The economics of collectibles and art markets have been studied extensively over the past several decades [2,6,18]. In the recent years, efforts have been made to study the economics of NFTs from various perspectives such as pricing [5], returns [19] and investment risk [12]. Despite these efforts, the role of ratings and reviews in art, collectible, or NFT marketplaces remains under-explored.

A number of recently proposed blockchain platforms [8,10] use reputation systems to properly incentivize correct behavior by the platform users. Steemit, a blogging and social media platform, has its own tokens which are used to incentivize users to post quality content [17]. Relevant, a news-sharing and discussion platform, introduces the concept of "reputation contexts" which allow users to earn reputation for different categories of content (e.g. politics, sports, technology, etc.) which allows users to specialize in and earn reputation for their expertise in specific categories [4]. In Steemit, curators (users who upvote content) are rewarded with tokens based on the performance of the content they upvote [17]. In Relevant, users can predict the performance of content they upvote and earn tokens based on their predictions. A few academic papers have also proposed blockchain-based review systems. A reputation-based system for IoT marketplaces has been proposed where device owners gain reputation when data consumers use their data and leave positive reviews [10].

On the academic side, a few rating and review systems have been proposed, including one which uses control products with known quality to randomly test reviewer honesty/ability [3]. Implementing this kind of "mystery shopper" approach for NFT marketplaces, though, is challenging because it's difficult to introduce a control product with a determined quality when the quality in question is subjective. It has also been suggested that user ratings could potentially enhance the transparency and trustworthiness of data in a decentralized data marketplace for smart cities [15]. We believe the in-depth analysis in this paper helps support this claim. Most similar to our work, one solution leverages Lina.Review [1], a blockchain-based review system, to implement a reputation system with two classes of users: *Helpers*, who are paid for high-quality reviews and *Common Users*, who are promoted to Helpers based on their high-quality reviews [7]. This solution, however, relies solely on likes to determine review quality (rather than sale price or some other ground truth metric, as our proposed solution does) and lacks a satisfying incentive analysis. ReviewChain [20], a decentralized blockchain-based review system, ensures the authenticity and integrity of reviews by maintaining singular identities for reviewers and confirming product purchase by reviewers, while our study focuses on different aspects - namely quality of reviews and product ranking.

To the best of our knowledge, our solution is the first decentralized rating and review system for NFT marketplaces that incentivizes high-quality sellers to use the platform and reviewers to provide unbiased and high-quality reviews.

3   Proposed Architecture

3.1   Use of Blockchain

Although our proposed architecture is blockchain-based, any transparent, publicly auditable, and immutable ledger with smart contract-like capabilities is suitable for our purpose. Governance decisions regarding the choice of consensus mechanism, participants in the consensus process, and related matters are entirely at the discretion of system designers.

3.2   Roles and Concepts

The entity that owns the NFT marketplace and the associated review system is referred to as the *authority*. Prior to deploying the system, the authority selects a set of *areas of expertise* that are relevant to the marketplace's offerings. For example, if the marketplace specializes in gaming-related NFTs, the areas of expertise may include art, music, first-person shooter (FPS) games, etc. Entities who list NFTs for sale on the marketplace are known as *sellers* and can include individual artists and/or authorized agents working on behalf of artists.

At the core of the review system are *reviewers*, who are responsible for evaluating the products listed on the marketplace as well as endorsing/reporting other reviewers. Through these actions, reviewers earn *expertise* points in the area(s) of expertise relevant to their actions. Expertise is a non-negative numerical value that quantifies the value a reviewer's opinions have in a particular area of expertise. The higher a reviewer's expertise score, the more impact their choices have on the system. At any given time t, the top k reviewers with the highest expertise in a particular area are considered *experts* of that area. Thus, once the system is deployed, participants may enter or exit the pool of experts over time.

3.3   Pre-deployment (Off-Chain) Phase

Prior to deploying the system, the authority selects the areas of expertise as well as the initial set of experts in each of those areas. The initial set of experts begin with a pre-determined high expertise score in their area of expertise whereas all other reviewers join the system with zero expertise in all areas. It is important to emphasize that the authority's involvement is confined to the pre-deployment phase. After the completion of this phase, no further actions are required from the authority to maintain the system.

3.4   Post-deployment (On-Chain) Phase

The post-deployment phase is considered per-asset, and involves the entire life cycle of an asset on the marketplace including admission control, marketplace listing, and sale. We refer to the entire life cycle of an asset as one *round*. Each round comprises of a total of eleven steps that can be categorized into *pre-listing*, *pre-sale* and *post-sale*. We now describe each step in detail.

Pre-listing. The pre-listing period, exclusive to experts in the relevant areas, focuses on admission control, i.e., determining whether the asset should be eli-

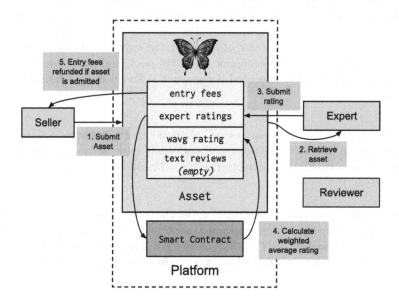

Fig. 2. Steps involved in the pre-listing period.

gible for listing on the marketplace. The various steps involved in the pre-listing period are depicted in Fig. 2. It consists of the following steps:

Step 1. The process begins when a seller, who has been approved by the authority, submits an asset to the marketplace. As our primary focus is on the review system, the specific details of the seller approval process are left to the authority. In addition to the asset itself, the seller indicates one or more *area tags* that are applicable to the asset and also stakes an *entry fee* stipulated by the marketplace. These area tags are used to identify the relevant set of experts responsible for evaluating the asset. The entry fee serves as a deterrent against spam and is forfeited if the asset fails to pass the admission control.

Step 2. Once the seller submits the asset, it is assigned to all the experts in the corresponding areas based on the specified area tags.

Step 3. Experts are given a predetermined amount of time to submit a numerical rating of the asset, say, on a scale from 0 to 5. The rating provided by expert i is denoted as r_i. Experts also have the option to submit text reviews in addition to the rating, allowing them to express their opinions about the asset in detail. Experts may opt to commit to a rating utilizing cryptographic techniques, withholding disclosure of the rating they committed to until the expiration of the designated time window.

Step 4. Upon the expiration of the designated time window, the smart contract calculates the weighted average numerical rating, denoted as $\bar{r}$, using the expertise scores of each expert as the respective weights.

Step 5. The smart contract makes the decision regarding the admission of the asset to the marketplace by comparing $\bar{r}$ with a minimum rating threshold (*thresh*) established by the authority. The asset is admitted if $\bar{r} \geq thresh$, and rejected otherwise. In the case of rejection, the entry fee staked by the seller is forfeited and added to the economic incentive pool, and the round ends. The subsequent steps are only executed if the asset is successfully admitted to the marketplace.

Pre-sale. During the pre-sale period, all non-expert reviewers are provided with the chance to review the asset and optionally endorse reviews contributed by other reviewers. Figure 3 depicts the steps involved. We now describe each step in detail:

Step 6. The admitted asset is displayed under the sales listing in decreasing order of $\bar{r}$, i.e., if asset a_1 has a higher weighted average rating than asset a_2, then a_1 is listed first, followed by a_2. Once the asset has been listed on the marketplace, it becomes accessible to all participants, including potential reviewers.

Step 7. Reviewers have the choice to submit a text review expressing their personal opinions about the asset, and/or make predictions about its relative sales performance (i.e, its objective popularity). The exact method of providing the relative sales performance prediction is left to the marketplace. For example, one viable method could involve reviewers ranking the currently listed assets based on their predicted popular demand from least to most popular. For resilience against Sybil attacks, the reviewers are also required to stake a nominal amount (chosen by the marketplace) while submitting reviews and/or predictions, that will be refunded after a stipulated time unless spam activity has been detected.

Step 8. Once a reviewer submits their review of the asset, experts corresponding to the relevant area(s) can retrieve the review, and optionally *endorse* it as described in the next step.

Step 9. Optionally, reviewers may *endorse* text reviews by other reviewers. All reviewers, regardless of their expertise level, are allocated a stipulated amount of *endorsement power* per asset, as determined by the authority. In this paper, we will consider the model where each reviewer is granted exactly one endorsement to utilize per asset that will expire if left unused. Thus, reviewers have the option to endorse a single text review (excluding their own) for each asset. Endorsements affect the way reviewers gain expertise in two ways:

    1. Expertise Gain by the Endorsee. While all reviewers have the ability to make endorsements, endorsements from experts result in the endorsee gaining some expertise in the corresponding area(s). The amount of expertise gained by the endorsee is determined by two factors: the expertise score of the endorsing expert, and the difference in expertise between the expert and the endorsee.

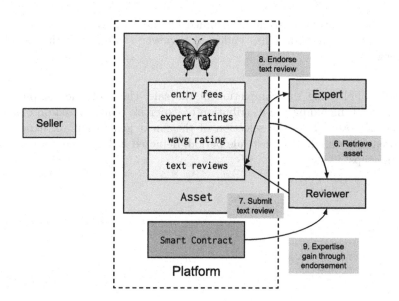

Fig. 3. Steps involved in the pre-sale period.

Mathematically, the expertise gained by a reviewer r due to an endorsement from expert e, denoted as $\Delta(r, e)$, can be represented as

$$\Delta(r, e) = mingain(exp_e) + addgain(max(0, exp_e - exp_r)) \qquad (1)$$

where exp_i is the expertise of person i, and $mingain()$ and $addgain()$ are functions defined by the authority that calculate the minimum expertise gain and the additional expertise gain respectively. Therefore, the minimum expertise gain is determined by the expertise score of the endorsing expert, and any additional expertise gain depends on the difference in expertise score between the endorsing expert and the endorsee.

2. *Expertise Gain by Investors.* Endorsements act as *investments* made by the endorser in the endorsee. By making this investment, the endorser establishes a stake and gains a proportionate fraction of the expertise acquired by the endorsee in subsequent rounds. The introduction of investments within the system is intended to incentivize experts to identify and endorse reviewers who are likely to consistently perform well over time, thus helping the system in identifying high-quality reviewers who eventually may progress to become experts themselves. Since an endorsement by an expert results in an expertise gain for the endorsee, all investors that invested in the endorsee up until the previous round will gain expertise proportional to their "share" of investment. However, to prevent gaming of the system, you cannot gain investment dividends from your own subsequent endorsements. Mathematically, the expertise gain by investor i due to a reviewer r being endorsed by an expert e can be represented as

$$dividend(i, r, e) = \frac{c_1 \times \Delta(r, e) \times invshare_r^i}{\sum_{j \in R} invshare_r^j} \qquad (2)$$

where c_1 is a positive constant determined by the authority, $invshare_r^i$ is the number of times investor i has endorsed reviewer r, and R is the set of all reviewers.

Post-sale. Following the completion of the sale, the post-sale computations are performed, including the distribution of expertise points based on observed sales metrics, as well as the selection of the "next generation" of experts for the subsequent round. The post-sale period, depicted in Fig. 4, comprises of the following steps:

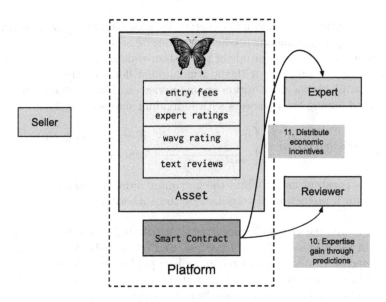

Fig. 4. Steps involved in the post-sale period.

Step 10. Once the sale has completed, based on the observed sales metrics, the system calculates a measure of how wrong the "collective judgement" of the system was about the popular demand of the asset. However, the exact way of comparing the popular demand of two assets depends on the sales method used.[1] Therefore, we assume for simplicity that the authority chooses some way to obtain the observed popular demand denoted as $demand_a \in [0,1]$ of asset a from some sale metric(s) of its choice. Furthermore, we also assume that the popular demand predictions made by each reviewer r can be converted in a similar fashion to $prediction_a^r \in [0,1]$ as well. Then, the individual prediction error of reviewer r on asset a can be calculated as

$$error(r, a) = (demand_a - prediction_a^r)^2 \tag{3}$$

and the system-wide prediction error of asset a, denoted by $\varepsilon(a)$, can be calculated as

$$\varepsilon(a) = \frac{\sum_{r \in R} error(r, a) \times exp_r^2}{\sum_{r \in R} exp_r^2} \tag{4}$$

where R is the set of all reviewers. The system-wide prediction error of asset a quantifies the extent to which the review system's collective judgment deviated from the actual popular demand for asset a. This measurement serves as the basis

---

[1] For instance, if two assets are sold at predetermined prices without quantity restrictions (e.g. digital copies of games), the gross sales revenue serves as a suitable measure for comparing their sales performance. In the case of assets sold through auctions, the final sale prices can be utilized as a metric.

for determining the total amount of expertise to be distributed among the reviewers who participated in making predictions. The size of the rewards pool increases proportionally with the magnitude of the system-wide prediction error, meaning that the greater its disparity with the true popular demand, the larger the pool of rewards available for distribution among reviewers. Finally, the rewards pool is distributed among the reviewers with individual shares defined as:

$$predshare(r, a) = \begin{cases} 0 & \text{if } error(r, a) \geq \varepsilon(a) \\ \frac{1}{max(c_2, error(r,a))} & \text{otherwise} \end{cases} \quad (5)$$

where c_2 is a constant used to limit the maximum number of shares any reviewer can obtain for a prediction, determined by the authority.

Step 11. Finally, the economic incentive is distributed to the experts that participated in the admission control process, and (optionally) the reviewers that gained expertise through endorsements and/or prediction. The economic incentive pool can be sourced from any forfeited entry fees from prior rounds, and/or some percentage of the gross revenue from the sales.

Checks and Balances System. While having an expert pool with special privileges can provide some protection against spam and malicious entities, it also requires us to actively identify and penalize malicious experts to ensure the proper functioning of the system. As the system works on inflationary economics in terms of expertise, incorrect or poor decisions may cause an expert to fall behind others over time, resulting in their removal from the expert pool. However, this process is slow and not sufficient to penalize all types of malicious actions, such as collusion.

To minimize the impact of malicious experts, we introduce the concept of periodic peer reviews. During these reviews, a majority vote among the experts can penalize a misbehaving expert by "burning" some or all of their expertise, effectively removing them from the expert pool. The transparency of the blockchain enables the entire history of actions by each expert to be publicly auditable, facilitating this process. Furthermore, this system of checks and balances also incentivizes experts to endorse other high-quality reviewers. However, it is important to note that the effectiveness of this checks and balances system depends heavily on the integrity of the initial set of experts. Therefore, it is crucial to have a majority (at least over 50%, preferably higher) of honest experts within the initial set. We also discuss the effects of having a checks and balances system on the correctness of the architecture in Sect. 4.2.

4   Evaluation

We analyze the proposed architecture by studying how various design parameters impact the selection of expert reviewers over time. In particular, we focus on the interplay between two reviewer skill-sets: the ability to subjectively assess the quality of an asset, and the ability to predict popular demand for an asset. We rely on numerical simulations to study these behaviors. Our choice of simulations is motivated by the complexity of the system, which makes it challenging to completely model mathematically, and the difficulty of conducting real-world studies on a scale comparable to that of an online NFT marketplace. Numerical simulations provide us with a way to estimate the system behavior at scale while allowing us to simplify the mathematics involved.

We begin our analysis by considering the simplified scenario in which all participants act *honestly*, i.e., perform actions to the best of their knowledge and abilities. We draw conclusions about the system behavior based on this scenario before considering the more general case where some participants may act maliciously. We then determine whether our conclusions hold in the face of such behavior.

4.1   Simulation with Honest Participants

Assumptions. Each asset a is assumed to have two hidden intrinsic properties[2] that stay constant throughout the simulation:

1. Quality, $q_a \in [0,1]$
2. Popular Demand, $d_a \in [0,1]$

Similarly, each reviewer r is assumed to have two hidden intrinsic properties that stay constant throughout the simulation:

1. Quality Estimation Ability (QEA), $qea_r \in [0,1]$
2. Popular Demand Prediction Ability (PDPA), $pdpa_r \in [0,1]$

Ideally, the authority should have the ability to specify a *slope parameter* within the range of $(-\infty, 0]$. This parameter determines the relative importance assigned to Quality Estimation Ability (QEA) compared to Popular Demand Prediction Ability (PDPA) when selecting reviewers to become experts. For instance, as shown in Fig. 5, when the slope is set to 0, the final set of experts ideally consists of reviewers with the highest QEA. In contrast, as the slope approaches $-\infty$, the final set of experts should ideally consist of reviewers with the highest PDPA. By adjusting the slope parameter, the authority can fine-tune the selection criteria for experts based on the desired emphasis between QEA and PDPA. Throughout the remaining analysis, we assume a slope parameter of -1, which assigns equal weightage to both QEA and PDPA. In this case, the final set of experts ideally comprises the dots located closest to the top right corner of the figure, i.e., points to the right of the diagonal orange line in Fig. 5.

---

[2] We use two different metrics because critic consensus and popular opinion can often diverge significantly. A notable example of a review system employing this concept is Rotten Tomatoes, which displays separate "Tomatometer" and Audience scores to capture this disparity.

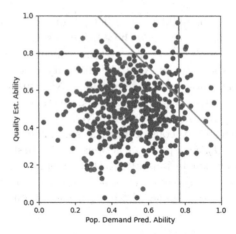

Fig. 5. A randomly drawn initial population of 500 reviewers, with red dots denoting the initial set of experts. The blue, magenta, and orange lines represent slope parameters of 0, $-\infty$, and -1 respectively. The ideal final expert set comprises the dots positioned above and/or to the right of the selected slope line. (Color figure online)

Simulation. At the beginning of the simulation, the QEA and PDPA values of each reviewer are randomly sampled from a normal distribution as shown in Fig. 5. A subset of reviewers is randomly chosen to form the initial expert set and is assigned an expertise value of 100,000, whereas everyone else starts with zero expertise. We also randomly sample the Quality and Popular Demand of each asset.

Each round in the simulation corresponds to the marketplace life cycle of one asset, as described in Sect. 3.4. Since we are interested in how the system selects the final expert set, we consider only those products that make it through the admission control process.

We assume that a reviewer's text review of an asset a corresponds to their estimate of q_a, and is denoted as $rev_a^r \in [0, 1]$. The magnitude of error of this estimation depends on the QEA of the reviewer. Concretely, rev_a^r is randomly drawn from the truncated triangular distribution with peak q_a and left and right intercepts determined by qea_r but truncated to the range [0,1]. Thus, the higher the QEA of a reviewer, the more likely rev_a^r will be closer to q_a. Similarly, a reviewer's sales demand prediction of an asset is assumed to be their estimate of d_a. As earlier, $pred_a^r$ is randomly drawn from the truncated triangular distribution with peak d_a and left and right intercepts determined by $pdpa_r$ but truncated to the range [0,1]. It is assumed that all participants of the system produce text reviews and popular demand predictions for all assets.

After the completion of text reviews, we proceed to simulate the endorsement process. Since we are considering the case where all participants are honest, we assume that each participant will attempt to endorse the review that best aligns with their own assessment. Concretely, each reviewer r endorses the reviewer r' that minimizes $|rev_a^r - rev_a^{r'}|$. For each endorsement, we keep track of the expertise gain and investment updates as described in Sect. 3.4.

Finally, we simulate the sale of the product. To incorporate market volatility, the sale demand metric is assumed to vary somewhat randomly around the Popular Demand of the asset, simulated using zero-mean Gaussian noise. Then, we calculate and distribute expertise based on the predictions made by the reviewers as described in Sect. 3.4. We then move on to the next round of simulation, repeating the process with a new asset.

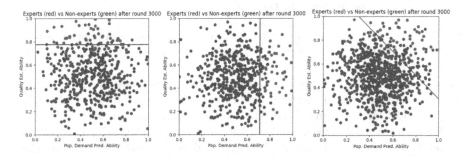

Fig. 6. Initial and final expert sets with expertise gain enabled from (i) endorsements only (i.e, *slope* = 0), (ii) popular demand predictions only (i.e, *slope* ≈ −∞), and (iii) both sources (i.e, *slope* = −1). The convergence behavior was observed even with new reviewers joining the system periodically.

Experiments and Results. First, we tested the behavior of the system with expertise gain from exactly one of the two sources, i.e., endorsements or popular demand predictions. This is effectively similar to setting the slope parameter to zero or −∞ respectively.

As seen in Fig. 6(i), with the expertise gain from Popular Demand prediction set to zero, the final expert pool after 3000 rounds consists of the reviewers with the highest QEAs. In particular, we discovered an interesting trend in the simulations: even when the initial set of experts is only "reasonably" good in terms of their QEA, with a sufficient number of rounds, the final expert set consists of mostly the reviewers with the highest QEA. To investigate this phenomenon further, we varied the minimum Quality Estimation Ability of the initial set of experts between 0.1 and 0.9 in steps of 0.1, and repeated the simulation 10 times for each setting. The results, consolidated in Fig. 7, indicate that the quality of the initial expert list does not necessarily determine the quality of the system. In other words, past a threshold of rounds, the system "self-corrects" by selecting highly skilled experts if all the initial experts have a QEA of at least 0.4. Similar trends were observed in experiments that allowed expertise gain from popular demand predictions alone, as illustrated in Fig. 6(ii).

Upon enabling expertise gain from both review endorsements and popular demand predictions, it was observed that the final expert pool predominantly consisted of reviewers positioned in the top right corner of the system, indicating high levels of both QEA and PDPA. This "convergence phenomenon" was consistently observed even when new reviewers joined the system over time, as

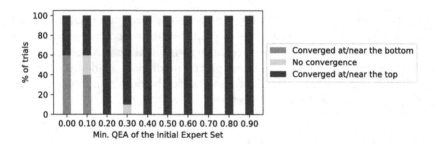

Fig. 7. Convergence behavior of the system with expertise gain from popular demand prediction set to 0. Figure 6(i) provides an illustrative example of convergence at/near the top.

illustrated in Fig. 6(iii). Therefore, based on empirical observations, we conclude that the system is able to select the final expert set by considering a combination of QEA and PDPA, despite these values being hidden from the system.

We then turned our focus to the question of how well the system selects the actual final expert set as compared to the ideal final expert set. To study this, we systematically varied the minimum QEA of the initial set of experts from 0.1 to 0.9 in increments of 0.1. For each setting, we repeated the simulation 10 times and recorded the average *combined score* of the actual and ideal final expert sets. In this context, the combined score is obtained by taking the mean of the QEA and PDPA values, as a slope parameter of −1 gives both factors equal importance. The summarized results are presented in Table 1.

Table 1. Mean combined score ($= \frac{QEA+PDPA}{2}$) of Actual vs Ideal (best 50) final expert set, compared to the initial expert set.

Min. Quality Est. Ability →	0.0	0.1	0.2	0.3	0.4	0.5	0.6	0.7	0.8	0.9
Initial Expert Set	0.50	0.48	0.47	0.58	0.57	0.59	0.6	0.64	0.72	0.72
Ideal Final Expert Set	0.76	0.77	0.73	0.76	0.78	0.78	0.77	0.76	0.78	0.80
Actual Final Expert Set	0.57	0.61	0.58	0.64	0.72	0.71	0.72	0.72	0.72	0.70

Table 1 reveals an interesting trend. When the initial set of experts has a minimum QEA of 0.3 or lower, the resulting final expert set demonstrates a significantly lower mean combined score compared to the ideal final expert set. Similarly, at the other extreme, when the initial set of experts has a minimum QEA of 0.8 or higher, the resulting final expert set performs at the same level as, or sometimes even worse than, the initial expert set. Between the two extremes, we identify a "sweet spot" for the minimum QEA of the initial expert set within the range [0.4, 0.6]. In this range, the actual final expert sets exhibit substantially higher quality than the initial set. Furthermore, the mean combined score of the actual final expert set is consistently close to that of the ideal final expert set.

4.2   Simulation with Potentially Malicious Participants

In the previous section, we made the assumption that all participants in the system would act honestly. However, in real-world deployments, this is never the case. To comprehensively examine the risks posed by malicious participants, we developed a threat model that considers a wide range of different malicious actions that participants could perform. We then analyzed the negative impact each malicious action can have on the system, the incentives driving such behavior, the safeguards in place to discourage such actions, and the scope and potential consequences of each malicious action based on the incentives and safeguards identified. Based on the detailed analysis provided in the full version of this paper[3], we concluded that the most significant malicious action deserving in-depth study is the act of reviewers engaging in selfish endorsements. This pertains to expert or non-expert reviewers endorsing text reviews for motives other than genuine alignment with their own views. Specifically, we focus on the following two questions:

1. Does adopting a selfish endorsement strategy provide long-term benefits for experts compared to utilizing an honest endorsement strategy?
2. How does the endorsement strategy employed by non-expert reviewers affect the convergence of the system?

Selfish Endorsement Strategies. We start by defining the following selfish endorsement strategies:

1. *Lazy Endorsement.* This strategy involves endorsing a randomly chosen text review without considering its quality.
2. *Endorse Another Expert.* Under this strategy, the reviewer intentionally endorses another expert to either maintain the *status quo* within the expert pool or potentially increase their own future investment dividends.
3. *Endorse a Poor Reviewer.* In this strategy, the reviewer purposely endorses a reviewer who exhibits low quality or competence, with the intention of preventing them from accumulating enough expertise to challenge the status quo within the expert pool.
4. *No Endorsement.* This strategy involves refraining from endorsing any review, thereby denying any reviewer the opportunity to gain expertise through the endorsement.

Experiments and Results. We conducted a series of experiments by varying the percentage of honest experts from 10% to 90%. The remaining experts were assigned different combinations of the four selfish strategies outlined previously. For each experiment, we recorded the average final expertise of the honest experts and experts employing any of the four selfish strategies. These

---

[3] The full version can be found at arXiv: https://arxiv.org/abs/2307.15768

Fig. 8. Final average expertise by strategy. For each experiment, we selected the selfish strategy that yielded the highest average final expertise and plotted it alongside the average final expertise of the honest experts.

results are consolidated in Fig. 8. From the figure, it is evident that the honest strategy consistently outperforms every analyzed selfish strategy in the long run. Additionally, the other selfish endorsement strategies only offer marginal improvements over not endorsing any review at all. Based on these empirical findings, we can now answers the questions posed earlier.

Firstly, the analysis of the four selfish endorsement strategies reveals that none of them offer any long-term benefits to the experts. On the contrary, the simulations clearly show that experts who endorse honestly have a significant advantage over those employ selfish endorsement strategies. Secondly, similar to experts, non-expert reviewers who employ an honest endorsement strategy were observed to outperform those who adopted selfish strategies.

Based on our analysis, we can conclude that the investment concept serves as an effective safeguard against reviewers engaging in selfish endorsements, which is the primary malicious action that participants can undertake within the system. Therefore, the results obtained in Sect. 4.1, which were based on the assumption of honest participants, can be applied more broadly to scenarios where the majority of experts are not malicious.

5 Conclusion

We have introduced a decentralized review system specifically designed for marketplaces that deal with highly scarce and highly resellable products, particularly focusing on NFT marketplaces. However, it is important to note that the proposed review system can be applied to any marketplace that involves the sale of extremely scarce products with significant resale potential. This can include various assets typically auctioned at specialized platforms or auction houses. The fundamental principles and mechanisms of our review system can be adapted and tailored to suit the specific characteristics and dynamics of different marketplaces, ensuring transparency, credibility, and reliability in evaluating and assessing the products being traded.

Future work could explore the implementation and deployment of such a system on a practical platform and evaluate with real users. Extensions to domains beyond art or game-related NFT marketplaces may also be of interest.

Acknowledgements. This research was funded by the Sony Research Award Program. This paper has been edited with the assistance of ChatGPT. We certify that ChatGPT was not utilized to produce any technical content, and we accept full responsibility for the contents of the paper.

References

1. Lina review - lina network. https://lina.network/lina-review/. Accessed 17 Dec 2022
2. Agnello, R.J.: Investment returns and risk for art: evidence from auctions of American paintings. Eastern Econ. J. **28**(4), 443–463 (2002). https://www.jstor.org/stable/40325391, publisher: Palgrave Macmillan Journals
3. Avyukt, A., Ramachandran, G.S., Krishnamachari, B.: A decentralized review system for data marketplaces. In: IEEE International Conference on Blockchain and Cryptocurrency, ICBC 2021, Sydney, Australia, May 3–6, 2021, pp. 1–9. IEEE (2021). https://doi.org/10.1109/ICBC51069.2021.9461149
4. Balasanov, S.: Technical overview of relevant protocols (2018)
5. Dowling, M.: Is non-fungible token pricing driven by cryptocurrencies? Financ. Res. Lett. **44**, 102097 (2022). https://www.sciencedirect.com/science/article/pii/S1544612321001781
6. Frey, B.S.: Art markets and economics: introduction. J. Cultural Econ. **21**(3), 165–173 (1997). https://www.jstor.org/stable/41810633, publisher: Springer
7. Glenski, M., Pennycuff, C., Weninger, T.: Consumers and curators: browsing and voting patterns on reddit. IEEE Trans. Comput. Soc. Syst. **4**(4), 196–206 (2017). https://doi.org/10.1109/TCSS.2017.2742242
8. Hasan, O., Brunie, L., Bertino, E.: Privacy-preserving reputation systems based on blockchain and other cryptographic building blocks: a survey. ACM Comput. Surv. **55**(2), 32:1–32:37 (2023). https://doi.org/10.1145/3490236. https://doi.org/10.1145/3490236
9. Hu, N., Liu, L., Zhang, J.: Do Online Reviews Affect Product Sales? The Role of Reviewer Characteristics and Temporal Effects. Inf. Technol. Manage. **9**, 201–214 (2008). https://doi.org/10.1007/s10799-008-0041-2
10. Javaid, A., Zahid, M., Ali, I., Khan, R.J.U.H., Noshad, Z., Javaid, N.: Reputation system for IoT data monetization using blockchain. In: Barolli, L., Hellinckx, P., Enokido, T. (eds.) BWCCA 2019. LNNS, vol. 97, pp. 173–184. Springer, Cham (2020). https://doi.org/10.1007/978-3-030-33506-9_16
11. Kalra, A., Stecklow, S., Stecklow, S.: Special Report: Amazon copied products and rigged search results to promote its own brands, documents show. Reuters, October 2021
12. Karim, S., Lucey, B.M., Naeem, M.A., Uddin, G.S.: Examining the interrelatedness of NFTs, DeFi tokens and cryptocurrencies. Financ. Res. Lett. **47**, 102696 (2022). https://www.sciencedirect.com/science/article/pii/S1544612322000253

13. Le Merrer, E., Morgan, B., Trédan, G.: Setting the Record Straighter on Shadow Banning. In: IEEE INFOCOM 2021 - IEEE Conference on Computer Communications, pp. 1–10, May 2021. https://doi.org/10.1109/INFOCOM42981.2021.9488792. iSSN: 2641-9874

14. Ng, J.: Most Popular NFT Marketplaces by Market Share (2023). https://www.coingecko.com/research/publications/market-share-nft-marketplaces

15. Ramachandran, G.S., Radhakrishnan, R., Krishnamachari, B.: Towards a decentralized data marketplace for smart cities. In: IEEE International Smart Cities Conference, ISC2 2018, Kansas City, MO, USA, September 16–19, 2018, pp. 1–8. IEEE (2018). https://doi.org/10.1109/ISC2.2018.8656952

16. Soper, S.: Amazon Doles Out Freebies to Juice Sales of Its Own Brands. Bloomberg.com, October 2018

17. Steem, J.: Steem: an incentivized, blockchain-based, public content platform (2017)

18. Stoller, M.A.: The economics of collectible goods. J. Cultural Econ. 8(1), 91–104 (1984). https://www.jstor.org/stable/41811143, publisher: Springer

19. Umar, Z., Gubareva, M., Teplova, T., Tran, D.K.: Covid-19 impact on NFTs and major asset classes interrelations: insights from the wavelet coherence analysis. Financ. Res. Lett. 47, 102725 (2022). https://www.sciencedirect.com/science/article/pii/S1544612322000496

20. Wang, K., Zhang, Z., Kim, H.S.: Reviewchain: smart contract based review system with multi-blockchain gateway. In: 2018 IEEE International Conference on Internet of Things (iThings) and IEEE Green Computing and Communications (GreenCom) and IEEE Cyber, Physical and Social Computing (CPSCom) and IEEE Smart Data (SmartData), pp. 1521–1526 (2018). https://doi.org/10.1109/Cybermatics_2018.2018.00256

21. Zhu, F., Zhang, X.M.: Impact of online consumer reviews on sales: the moderating role of product and consumer characteristics. J. Marketing 74(2), 133–148 (2010)

Bringing Web 3.0 and DAO into Democratic Class: A study of Pedagogy in Higher Education

Hanlin Ma[(⊠)] [iD], Lu Li, Yirui Wu, and Jiaqi Wang

Suzhou University of Science and Technology, Suzhou, Jiangsu, China
fanfan2011cn2000@gmail.com

Abstract. Blockchain technology introduces a paradigm shift into higher education, presenting opportunities for innovative transformations in human organization and democratic operations. Education-based Decentralized Autonomous Organizations (DAOs) on Web 3.0 are anticipated to instigate change across the spectrum, from classroom pedagogy to broader educational systems. Our research concentrates on the micro-level exploration of the merger between the decentralization principles of educational DAOs and traditional democratic classrooms. In the course of our experimental study, we analyze an experimental postgraduate course that uses a governing token to stimulate decision-making processes, empowering students with a participatory role that mirrors DAO operations. The implementation of popular DAO tools is discussed with the goal of crafting a classroom environment reflecting the decentralized decision-making structures intrinsic to DAOs. While we underscore the potential of decentralized teaching methodologies to enhance democratic education, we particularly focus on students as the primary facilitators of collective decision-making. According to our investigation, students showed a greater understanding and positivity towards decentralization than expected, suggesting that a suitable environment could boost positive behavior in class. Furthermore, in an architecturally decentralized class, a properly operational tokenomics could enhance classroom liberty, particularly for elite students, who might exert significant influence due to tokenomics and reward mechanisms.

Keywords: DAO · Democratic education · Blockchain for education

1 Introduction

In recent years, blockchain technology has emerged as a transformative force across various sectors, with higher education being no exception. The core value of blockchain technology resides in its inherent decentralization and transparency, which fosters a more democratic, equitable, and accountable system. By eliminating the need for central authorities, it empowers individuals and communities, reduces the potential for corruption, and promotes greater inclusivity and cooperation across diverse stakeholders. This decentralized nature of blockchain, alongside its inherent security, reliability, and data integrity, presents numerous benefits to higher educational institutions.

Q. Wang et al. (Eds.): ICBC 2023, LNCS 14206, pp. 21–37, 2023.
https://doi.org/10.1007/978-3-031-44920-8_2

The capabilities of blockchain not only signal a technological revolution but also instigate a reshaping of the organizational structures and operational methods in human societies. This shift is epitomized by Decentralized Autonomous Organizations (DAOs). Higher education is not immune to this metamorphosis. Both micro and macro aspects of higher education will be significantly influenced by these emergent organizational structures and instructional paradigms. Our research is committed to investigating from a micro perspective, particularly classroom teaching, the fusion of DAO's core principles with distinct educational philosophies. We have observed that democratic education innately aligns with the decentralization espoused by DAOs and blockchain's core values. This amalgamation extends beyond a mere adoption of blockchain and internet technologies, aiding in our exploration of innovative educational models, as evidenced in the intricacies and operational modes of Ed3's core values.

To accomplish this objective, it is essential to delineate the fundamental concepts of decentralization. Further, by implementing exploratory classroom experiments and empirical research, we aim to determine the extent to which this integration realizes the application of decentralization and the current limitations and challenges it encounters. In our research, we examine a postgraduate course where a governing token is deployed to facilitate decision-making processes. This token is utilized in a voting mechanism for class debates, effectively offering students an active role in shaping the course's trajectory, thus simulating the operations of a DAO. Employing popular DAO tools such as Snapshot, Charmverse, and Metamask, we aim to create a classroom environment that mirrors the decentralized decision-making structures found in DAOs. To evaluate the effectiveness and degree of acceptance of this DAO-style governance, a comprehensive questionnaire is administered to the students upon the completion of the course. The aim is to assess the impact on students' diverse tiers of understanding, desire, and implementation regarding decentralization within democratic educational environments. Simultaneously, we intend to provisionally gauge the role of the amalgamation of DAO practices, principles, and democratic classrooms in this setting.

2   DAOs and Ed3

The advantages of applications derived from blockchain technology and other Web 3.0-based installations in higher education, can be fundamentally outlined via two perspectives: the progression of educational technology and the transformation of the organizational structure of the educational system.

Addressing the former perspective, a multitude of applications emerge that can be regarded as value-neutral tools, possessing the potential for seamless implementation within traditional educational settings. The tamper-proof characteristic of blockchain technology makes it an ideal tool for securing and validating qualifications, thereby enhancing trust and transparency in credential verification processes [1]. Institutions such as MIT have already initiated the process of issuing virtual academic credentials, thereby attesting to the efficacy and potential of blockchain in higher education [2].)

Beyond the aforementioned perspectives, a plethora of applications, intrinsically linked to the core values of blockchain technology, are prominently emerging in contemporary times. For instance, blockchain can facilitate the democratization of education by providing universal access to open educational resources [3]. The unalterable nature of this technology enables secure sharing of resources on a public network, promoting lifelong learning while concurrently reducing costs. A remarkable operation within this domain is the Decentralized Autonomous Organization (DAO) for education, which aligns with our focal theme. DAOs are digital entities constructed and functioning on smart-contract-based platforms. The governance aspect of DAOs has attracted considerable attention in academic research, as they are believed to offer a democratic platform that is accessible to individuals who align with their principles or stated objectives [4]. On a broader scale, DAOs for education serve the concept known as Education 3.0 (Ed3) [5].

Philosophically, Ed3 embodies a highly democratized and market-oriented form of education, where decisions regarding the distribution of capital resources, human resources, and knowledge resources are made by diverse stakeholders. These stakeholders include teachers, students, and others, such as investors in education. The composability of education would be enhanced, the construction of the curriculum and module combinations would create greater individuation of education for every individual student.

Technologically, the decision-making process within Ed3 is tokenized, employing smart contracts on blockchains, such as Ethereum. Building upon this foundational organizational structure and utilizing other autonomous decentralized software applications, traditional educational governance, typically controlled by an elite few, is supplanted. Consequently, the governance of education is driven by market forces and collective decision-making, paving the way for a more equitable and democratized educational landscape. Various organizations working with this model are DAOs for education [6].

The preceding surge in the crypto technology bull market was primarily focused on Decentralized Finance (DeFi), and within this framework, it remains debatable whether DAOs have transitioned into a phase of robust development. DAOs fundamentally emphasize production and construction, rather than finance. Present challenges associated with DAOs for education include excessive financialization (such as the "learning to earn" DeFi game); inadequate product implementation; and noticeable remnants of Education 2.0 (Ed2) (as characterized by Atish Mistry as "centralized platforms distributing education, such as Udemy, Skillshare, and Outschool").Nevertheless, these hurdles do not preclude us from investigating and scrutinizing existing, valuable operational models that bear resemblance to, or are related to DAOs that resonate with the principles of Education 3.0 (Ed3). In accordance with the insights provided by Scott Meyer and Vriti Saraf, four distinct characteristics of DAOs for education merit attention [6]:

1. DAOs for education operate on protocols that align with the blockchain, thereby automating a substantial portion of their operations.
2. DAOs for education encompass collective ownership, learning communities, social clubs, content curation, and asset creation. This contrasts with traditional cooperatives, which primarily concentrate on collective ownership of tangible products or assets, such as housing or specific goods.
3. While cooperatives typically adhere to a one-person-one-vote paradigm, DAOs for education possess the flexibility to innovate governance structures via an array of tokenomics and voting protocols.

4. DAOs for education establish stratified incentive structures using tokenomics that cater to an array of personal interests, such as earning, learning, producing, promoting, and networking, all consolidated within a singular platform.

Crypto, Culture & Society, DeveloperDAO, VectorDAO, MetricsDAO, ScribeDAO, Daokrayaki, among others, could be regarded as DAOs for education, in addition to fulfilling various functions such as knowledge sharing, training, job markets, project funding, and social engagement. Essentially, they constitute social communities that operate on platforms such as Discord and Twitter. United under specific shared values, these communities engage in knowledge sharing, provide job opportunities through a cryptocurrency-based bounty system, raise funds, and sponsor projects aligned with their guiding philosophy.

Given the burgeoning demand for developers in the Web 3.0 industry, the most influential learning DAOs are those tailored for developers. Hackathons are frequently organized globally by nearly all DAOs reliant on information technology. In this sphere, the influence of traditional higher education is difficult to discern. These DAOs offer a more liberal, democratic environment that directly connects learners to the industry. While it is challenging to discern the necessity of traditional educational institutions such as schools or universities within the framework of Ed3, practitioners based within these establishments may facilitate their integration through a process of transformation. Local teacher organizations, research communities, and student clubs all possess the potential to alter the functioning of education through DAOs.

In future, numerous macro and micro DAOs may exist within the educational spectrum, each possessing distinctive decision-making needs. Nevertheless, up until now, most decentralization endeavors in Ed3 have concentrated on educational management and resource allocation within education, while placing minimal emphasis on classroom teaching and pedagogy. This is an area where decision-making and choice also play a pivotal role in determining what knowledge needs to be learned, how knowledge is constructed in the classroom, and how the learning is evaluated. The operation of DAO may also play a useful role in this realm. The reason Ed3 proponents and practitioners seldom focus on this area is because physical classrooms are often omitted from their narratives. However, a shift towards the integration of traditional teaching systems with Ed3 could hold significant value. Given suitable conditions, the technological platforms and operational methods intrinsic to DAOs could instigate meaningful changes within traditional classrooms.

The integration of DAOs into classroom practice holds significant implications. Based on our prior discussions, there are two primary avenues for the implementation of blockchain in education:1. Employing it as a neutral tool; 2. Instigating an evolution of education, thereby overturning the old order dominated by the traditional education system. The first approach does not tap into the inherent value of blockchain, whereas the integration of blockchain and web 3.0 technology should ideally enact transformative changes in education. The second approach, while it more fully embraces the potential of blockchain, might be perceived as premature, radical, and too confined to specific areas of learning. Consequently, its acceptance within broader society remains a challenge.

A middle ground may assist those entrenched in the traditional education system to consider employing DAOs as a force for educational reform, capturing the humanistic values intrinsic to blockchain technology. By adopting a balanced approach, the core principles of decentralization, transparency, and autonomy embodied by blockchain can be used to enhance educational practice and governance, without negating the existing strengths of traditional educational systems.

3 What is Decentralization?

An educational movement committed to decentralizing the traditional education system is not new. Known as "democratic education" or "freedom-based education", the model is one in which students maintain autonomy over their learning content, method, and schedule. This concept has its roots in a diverse range of historical and philosophical traditions, such as the ancient Greek philosophers, Romantic thinkers like Rousseau and Froebel, the libertarian-anarchist tradition, the 19th century, American transcendentalist movement, and the free-school movement of the 20th century. Significant examples of the latter involve the Summerhill School, led by A. S. Neill, and the extensive establishment of free schools across the United States during the countercultural revolution of the 1960s and 1970s [13]. The democratic classroom stands as a significant sector within the educational spectrum that employs this freedom-based education paradigm.

In acknowledging that both democratic classrooms and DAOs operate under the paradigm of decentralization, there are three salient issues that require elucidation:

1. The essence of decentralization within the context of democratic classrooms.
2. The characteristics of decentralization inherent to DAOs.
3. The compatibility between these two forms of decentralization, along with the criteria for examining this compatibility.

Addressing these issues will enhance our comprehension of the decentralization paradigm as it applies in these two distinct, yet potentially complementary, contexts. Before embarking on the comparison, it is imperative to clarify the analytical framework of the concept of decentralization. According to Vitalik Buterin [14], there exist three dimensions of (de)centralization: Architectural (de)centralization, Political (de)centralization, and Logical (de)centralization. While these definitions have been designed for the realm of information technology, Buterin's instances of decentralization extend well beyond the computer world. Thus, we find it necessary to generalize these dimensions:

1. Architectural (de)centralization—How many "accounts" control the system?
2. Political (de)centralization—How many individual or organizational minds exert control over the system?
3. Logical (de)centralization—Do all users adhere to a standard operational design imposed by the creator of the system?

An instance cited by Buterin involves direct democracy, which he categorizes as politically decentralized, architecturally centralized, and logically centralized. The descriptor "politically decentralized" indicates a lack of control by a single individual or organization. "Architecturally centralized" implies that all decision makers operate within a single chamber or under a single "account", if this account fails or becomes canceled, the entire system collapses. "Logically centralized" refers to a system where all participants adhere to the rules set by the original creator of the system, hence maintaining a singular mode of operation.

In reference to blockchain technology, Buterin classifies it as politically and architecturally decentralized yet logically centralized. This characterization reflects the operational nature of the blockchain which, while being determined by multiple accounts (or computers) and controlled by diverse individuals or organizations, still requires all participants to conform to the protocols established by the system's originator. Prior to delving into the discourse surrounding the political (de)centralization attributes of democratic classrooms and DAOs for education, we aim briefly to assess the aspect of logical (de)centralization in this context. We posit that all classrooms under consideration would be logically decentralized, as the pedagogical approach within these classrooms remains stable, regardless of whether they exhibit political decentralization and architectural decentralization.

4   The Essence of Decentralization Within the Context of Democratic Classrooms

Democratic education demonstrates a broad spectrum of applications, spanning from micro-level classroom democracy to the idealized macro-level school-wide democracy. As per the aspirations of democratic education activists and theorists, there is even a call for transforming an entire nation's education system to align with democratic principles. This ambition parallels those pioneering Ed3 and the utilization of DAOs in education. However, the realization of democratic education encounters numerous theoretical and practical challenges, which limits its widespread implementation. Most manifestations of democratic education are restricted to micro-level classroom practices; hence, this study will focus primarily on decentralized pedagogy within democratic classrooms.

We shall draw from two instances to exemplify the feasibility of decentralization within democratic classrooms. The first case, "Teaching Assistant Training Program" (TATP), has been established by the Centre for Teaching Support & Innovation (CTSI) at the University of Toronto. Since 2002, this initiative has aimed at fostering democratic learning within classrooms for Teaching Assistants and Course Instructors at the Roberts Library. Additional teaching and learning workshops targeting TAs and instructors have been facilitated at both the UT Scarborough campus and UT Mississauga campus. The underlying aim of this TA training program is to cultivate democratic teaching and learning practices among TAs and students. It is designed to further facilitate the process of peer teaching and peer learning among students [15].

As illustrated in the report [15], the implementation of democratic classes within this project is confined to facilitating open discussions and peer learning, aiming to enhance the democratic competencies of TAs and students. Such competencies encompass understanding diversity, appreciating ambiguity and complexity, challenging assumptions, attentive and respectful listening, acknowledging persistent differences, fostering intellectual flexibility, recognizing connections, respecting experiences, embodying democratic habits, creating collective knowledge, effective communication, collaborative learning, widening comprehension and empathy, and the synthesis, integration, and transformation of ideas and actions. These skills represent the positive freedom essential for practicing democracy in constructing knowledge, a prerequisite for political decentralization.

However, these competencies should not be misconstrued as fully democratic; they align more accurately with critical thinking, particularly when class topics bear minimal relevance to politics. We can call this critical pedagogy rather than fully decentralized pedagogy such as "banking method" by Brazilian educator Paulo Freire [16]. It may be observed that when students are granted increased tangible political power within the classroom, the exercise of their action of positive freedom tends to diminish [15].

A fully realized democratic classroom should incorporate elements that engender and represent negative freedom. This implies the necessity for a relatively formalized collective decision-making process, such as voting, within the classroom. Moreover, students should consider this process with great care, given that the outcomes of such votes could directly influence their educational experiences. Consequently, Case 2 merits closer examination.

The case 2 to be considered is Ira Shor's "Utopia Course" at the City University of New York, serving working students. The relaxed external environment affords an opportunity for Shor to experiment with democratic education in a higher education setting. Unlike the Teaching TATP, Shor seeks to fully embody the philosophy of democratic education by transforming the classroom into a politically decentralized space, as opposed to merely decentralizing diverse thoughts. To this end, Shor not only utilizes discussions, but also provides students with test and assignment options that cater to their unique learning preferences. He also allows students "protest rights", practices contract grading or self-grading, permits students to address the teacher by their first name, and encourages students to co-construct knowledge [17].

It can be argued that Ira Shor's class represents a genuinely politically decentralized entity, despite the inherent authority that his status as a teacher might confer. Shor makes considerable efforts to minimize this element of centralization, by altering the seating arrangement between him and the students, by allowing students to address him by his first name, and by adopting a Socratic approach to questioning rather than a didactic teaching style. Nonetheless, it is challenging to eliminate the naturally centralized political characteristics of the traditional classroom in a practical implementation of classes akin to Shor's.

In summary, it is reasonable to assert that traditional democratic classrooms hold the potential to achieve political decentralization, though they fail to fulfill the requirements for architectural decentralization, largely due to their similarities with direct democracy. If the school decides to terminate the course, or if the instructor elects to discontinue the course, it would invariably cease. This underscores the inherent weakness of architectural centralization; if the "account" or the sole operating deployment of the work is compromised, or falls under the control of a malicious individual, the recovery of the system becomes significantly challenging. The same issue could arise with centralized educational platforms.

5 Different Democratic Classes with Regard to the Context of Decentralization

We now turn our attention to assessing the degree of decentralization exhibited by DAOs, specifically those intended for education. DAOs for education are architecturally and politically decentralized. This is presumed to be advantageous for these DAOs, given that the political landscape within cyberspace differs markedly from that of the physical world. But it is an oversimplification to conclude that classes of DAOs are more decentralized or better than democratic classes.

Discussing the divergence between the DAOs' realm and the physical educational world, it is noteworthy that DAOs are marked by a high degree of tribalism, partly in consequence of its anarchistic nature. Unlike citizens confined to physical locations under governmental regulations, inhabitants active in cyberspace are unrestricted by a tangible space that limits their access to various cyber domains—a mere click of a mouse allows for fluid transitions. Given this convenience of unrestricted movement, cyber residents are not obliged to harmonize with others who may not share their values, moral stances, or political ideologies. This circumstance eventually leads to the formation of internet tribes. The core members of these tribes likely have visited numerous communities before deciding to associate with one. Consequently, democracy within these tribes may be taken more seriously because cyberspace offers alternatives to "fighting" within a democratic system. These alternatives include leaving, to choose another tribe more aligned with their interests, or forking the community into separate entities unless compelling reasons exist to maintain the unity and growth of the community.

Thus, a class governed by a DAO for education may not necessarily demand stringent democratic engagement. Different teaching channels or websites are akin to small tribes, with the teacher, as the space's owner, likely adhering to traditional pedagogical practices in their interaction with students. Given the vast amount of content available online, the necessity to implement composability of content "within" their class may seem redundant. Reflecting on the definition of E3 as outlined in preceding sections of this paper, the composability it advocates may be best applied "outside the class". This discrepancy between the actual practices of DAOs for Ed3 and democratic classrooms could be considered their primary incongruity. However, the channels for communication between these two remain open.

The crucial question here is whether the organic nature of a Shor-style democratic class retains its significance in light of Ed3, and whether the introduction of architectural decentralization might enhance democratic education. In our opinion, the answer is "affirmative". Most of today's so-called DAOs for education appear to inadequately integrate the class system with tokenomics. The lack of innovative deployment of Web3 technology in pedagogy could explain why the "learn to earn" scheme often devolves into a financial narrative or merely generates memberships with little intrinsic value. In such a situation, when an individual earns tokens through 'learning,' which is often defined by simple processes of recording and testing, the primary incentive to proceed seems to be the potential for selling these tokens. It could be argued that the design philosophy of this system is fundamentally flawed because it undermines the core purpose of learning, which is to approach the truth and gain knowledge, skills and understanding. A democratic educator might refine this statement by emphasizing that the journey towards acquiring knowledge is equally deserving of consideration by the learner. This focus allows learners to understand the 'why' and 'what' of learning rather than just the 'what,' fostering a more holistic and purposeful learning experience.

Hence, it would be significant to imbue these DAO tokens with more functionality. When introducing innovation to education, three levels are of concern: the classroom level, the institutional level, and the more macro societal level. Likewise, for promoting Ed3, we may consider the class level, the DAO level, and a broader macro level. Implementing a tokenization operation at the classroom level (assuming that classes exist in Ed3) could be a feasible method for learners, who are likely minor stakeholders, to engage with the democratization of education and knowledge. This process could potentially forge strong connections with democratization efforts at other educational levels. Consequently, the economic value of these tokens would be reinforced by these more fundamental values.

Table 1. Decentralization statuses pertaining to the five distinct class types.

	critical thinking education	political decentralized education	architectural decentralized education	logically decentralized pedagogy
TATP Style Class	Y	N in organization level; N in class level	N	N
Shor Style Class	Y	N in organization level; Y in class level	N	N
General DAOs for Edu3	Y	Y in organization level; N in class level	Y	N
Edu3&Shor Style Class(ESSC)	Y	Y in organization level; Y in class level	Y	N
ESSC negative	Y	N in organization level; Y in class level	Y	N

To explore the fusion of Ed3 and democratic education, we propose a pedagogical model (Ed3&Shor Style Class, ESSC for short) that introduces tokenization into the democratic classroom, thereby transforming all procedures requiring collective decision-making. This includes the selection of lecture content, students' preferences for examination content, and voting to express support for discussion standpoints. The process of token distribution would be linked to the academic behavior and engagement of the students, as observed through their bounty applications and participation in classroom discussions, etc. With this mechanism, a sub-circuit of tokenomics would be established within the class. We maintain an open setting towards a more macro-level tokenomics in higher levels, potentially encapsulating this one and encouraging the development of more diversified and flexible rules within this ecosystem. An ESSC with negative attributes would constitute an isolated class, devoid of the context of decentralization at the school level or any broader macro level.

6   A Web3 and Democratic Class Simulating ESSC Negative

To suitably align with the constraints posed by the Chinese education system and the theme of the course, we have designed a class that simulates the ESSC negative while incorporating several distinct features. Here are the principal deviations from the ESSC negative model in our design:

1. Our governing token for the class will be deployed on the Ethereum blockchain's testnet, as opposed to the mainnet. This approach is motivated by several considerations: first, launching such a project on Ethereum would be prohibitively expensive, and we lack the necessary budget; second, there is no perceptible difference for students in terms of client-side operations; third, there is no compelling need for tokenomics with real economic value at the class level; and finally, it helps circumvent any potential risks stemming from school-level prohibitions.
2. In view of the cultural influences and prevalent class participation habits among Chinese students, the teacher's authority in our class will not be as significantly reduced as in Shor's class model.

The courses implementing our design are titled "Introduction to Dialectics of Nature" and are available to graduate students at Suzhou University of Science and Technology. These courses introduce foundational aspects of knowledge and knowledge production—concepts that can also be described as philosophical characteristics of science and its evolution—along with related philosophical topics on science and technology development. Given that the construction of knowledge within our course also signifies a form of knowledge production, the exercise of democracy in constructing knowledge within our course shows the mirror relationship between pedagogy and learning content. To outline our design, we will elucidate the Web 3.0 tools employed, tokenomics and the classroom governance involved.

Tools

Metamask is a browser extension that allows users to interact with decentralized applications (DApps) on the Ethereum blockchain. It serves as a digital wallet, enabling users to securely store, manage, and transfer Ethereum and other ERC-20 tokens. Metamask provides a user-friendly interface, making it easier for individuals to access and engage with the world of decentralized finance (DeFi) and blockchain-based applications.

Charmverse is a platform that integrates blockchain technology, specifically tokens and NFTs (Non-Fungible Tokens), into a community forum. We use it for delivering bounties.

Snapshot is a governance tool used by decentralized communities and projects. It allows token holders to vote on proposals, participate in decision-making processes, and shape the future direction of a project. Snapshot uses blockchain technology to ensure transparency, immutability, and security in voting processes.

Tokenomics

We will issue a batch of tokens, minted simultaneously and held by the classroom manager (a somewhat centralized approach). However, this approach is adopted for ease of management. As this study is limited to classroom management research and does not delve into the economic aspects of education.

The functions of these tokens are threefold: 1) to be used for voting governance; 2) to be issued as rewards for tasks (bounties); 3) to serve as a reference for tracking routine performance. The distribution of these tokens follows three methods: 1) as bounties; 2) to students participating in the voting; 3) to students participating in classroom management work (if there is a teaching assistant, this step is omitted). In the initial round of token distribution, class monitors from each group were delegated to distribute the tokens. However, due to unsatisfactory results, the distribution of tokens was transferred to the hands of the teaching assistants. Through the application of this tokenomics system, students can acquire greater governance over the class by actively participating. This process not only increases their agency but also enhances the likelihood of their preferences influencing the final examination content and subsequently improving their usual grades. The system thus fosters an environment where student engagement directly impacts their academic outcomes.

Classroom Governance

Online part:

1. Implemented on Charmverse, the main activities include forum discussions and bounties. Ways of earning bounties include: 1) Registration for topic discussion and debates (bounties are awarded after debating or other class speeches), 2) Distributed knowledge collection (bounties are confirmed after verification). Token distribution principles: In addition to acquiring bounties, everyone participating in the voting can receive a certain number of tokens. The bounties are significantly higher than the rewards for regular activities. Required tools: Metamask wallet, Charmverse (DAO governance tool)
2. Voting, implemented on Snapshot. The main work is off-chain voting. Voting subjects include: 1) Classroom topic resolution selection, 2) Selection of classroom lecture content, 3) Voting on classroom assessment topics (survey on classroom assessment content preferences). Required tools: Metamask wallet, Snapshot

Offline Part

The offline part includes special topic discussion and debate (in class), lecture, exams, etc.

Presentation Section: Each resolution has 3–4 rounds, each round is represented by a pro and con party from a group, presenting their stance and evidence, each presentation should be between 3 and 5 min.

Debate Section: Each resolution has one debate, proposed by a group with recommended pro and con debaters. The total time for debate is 15 min. The debate is conducted by taking turns, with an "answer then question" approach. Each representative has a total of 7.5 min, and each round of speaking time should not exceed 2 min. To encourage participation, students who join the debate without prior registration can receive a 50% additional bounty. The encourages students to facilitate the entire debate.

The lecture topics are designed to offer a variety of choices. There are 20 potential lectures that correspond to the course theme, exceeding the number of course hours. From these, students will select eight topics. The first six topics form a cohesive series centered around scientific methodology and the history of philosophy in science and technology. The remaining 14 lectures are more varied, encompassing philosophical discussions on cognitive science, blockchain, the metaverse, artificial intelligence, and other related themes.

7   The Examination of Decentralization Within the Simulated ESSC Negative

The implementation of a decentralized democratic classroom presents multiple challenges, involving students, teachers and institutions. This study will concentrate on the most crucial subjective viewpoint - the students', since they are the primary agents engaging in collective decision-making, a significant outcome for such a class. Our analysis will utilize the fundamental framework proposed by Morrison [13], focusing on the positive freedom exhibited by students in the classroom, given the pre-existing conditions of freedom in a democratic environment. Contrary to traditional democratic classrooms, our simulated ESSC negative model integrates web 3.0 technology and its associated political mechanisms, resulting in several notable advantages: 1. The anonymity provided in such a setting encourages a more robust exercise of freedom of speech and other forms of liberty; 2. The tokenomics model incentivizes active participation in class with the prospect of earning rewards.

We anticipate findings that extend beyond a simplistic answer such as "students lack behaviors indicative of positive freedom", given the innovative feature of decentralization introduced in this study. In order to accomplish this goal, we employ two types of assessment to scrutinize students' understanding, desires, and implementation levels concerning decentralization. The first is a comprehensive post-course survey covering diverse aspects of the students' experiences about decentralization. The second involves evaluating students' classroom performance through a combination of subjective evaluations by teachers and data on classroom participation.

Furthermore, we have established two control groups comprising two lecture courses at Campus A (with a total of 360 students) and two at Campus B (totaling 376 students). These groups employ similar teaching methodologies and content but differ in the curricular scheduling. Referred to as Group A and Group B, respectively, the former has its lecture content, except for the introduction and pedagogical courses, determined by student voting on Snapshot. Conversely, in Group B, the instructor determines the course's first half, with decision-making authority delegated to students for the remainder. Given the close alignment of classroom debates with previously covered content, the two groups also differ in the progress and continuity of debate topics. This arrangement aims to examine whether content continuity influences student engagement.

We disseminated the electronic questionnaire via social media, garnering 163 responses from Group A and 116 from Group B. The questionnaire consisted of 33 questions, 13 of which were directly related to students' understanding, desire, and implementation of various types of decentralization (table1). We classified the strength of these associations into three levels: weak, medium, and strong, and inferred students' positivity towards different types of decentralization (understanding, desire, implementation) based on their responses. The data for Groups A and B can be found in Fig. 1.

We classified decentralization according to Table 1 discussed earlier and defined critical thinking as a type of decentralization. While critical thinking does not fall into the categories of decentralization defined by Vitalik Buterin, it is associated with a diversity of values and a high degree of acceptance of rational thinking processes. We thus believe it can serve as a parameter expressing positive freedom. Additionally, to avoid excessively technical questions in the survey, all our questions employed common-sense language and therefore, might not precisely correlate with a specific type of decentralization. Consequently, some questions might relate to multiple types of decentralization simultaneously, but with varying degrees of correlation.

We notice that there is no significant difference between Group A and Group B. This suggests a strong commonality among students from both groups in their self-perception of understanding, desire, and implementation concerning various types of decentralization. According to the data, students seem to have a relatively higher understanding and acceptance of political decentralization and its value of this class. There is a comparatively lower desire for critical thinking and political decentralization, yet a certain interest and inclination towards architectural decentralization are demonstrated. Nevertheless, the level of implementation for all types of decentralization appears relatively low. Upon examining the lecture content selection and debate voting conditions of the control group, several noteworthy points emerge (Fig. 2):

1. Group B's voting rate for lecture content selection is lower than Group A's.
2. The voting rate and standard deviation of vote distribution for lecture content selection in Group A shows a trend of initial decline followed by a return to previous levels.
3. Even after opening up lecture content selection in the second half of the course, Group B still continued to select the next chapter in accordance with the original teaching order (Scientific Methodology and History of Science and Technology), demonstrating a rational exercise of positive freedom in choice. A relative rationality in choice was also observed in the third and fourth rounds of content selection in Group B. The selected lecture content on these two occasions were "The Rise of Modern Science (including a bit of Medieval Science content)" and "Dialectics of Nature after Socrates." Despite the teacher suggesting that students could select certain content if they wished to learn more about the related knowledge, there was no obligation for the students to heed the teacher's advice.

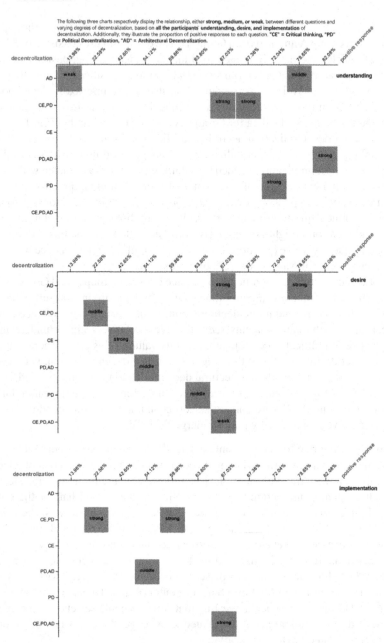

Fig. 1 Comparative analysis of three dimensions across diverse decentralization collections for all the students.

8 Discussion

Issue: Our observations suggest that, in contrast to a minority of proactive participants or 'elite students,' the majority of students exhibit a stronger inclination towards the implementation of negative freedom than positive freedom. This propensity remains robust despite the challenges posed by the deployment of blockchain technology and network instability. The classroom's sole objective for positive freedom is to cultivate students' capacity to contemplate various attributes of knowledge and technology in philosophy, yet this intent appears less appealing to many. Evidenced by lower voting rates for differing debate stances compared to lecture content selections, it seems that the requirements for positive freedom in this classroom setting may be overlooked or mis-construed as merely offering negative freedoms. Consequently, students tend to express limited interest in ballots demanding rational effort, favoring decisions that can be made impulsively.

Response: Upon reviewing the choices regarding lecture content made by Group A, as well as the responses to the survey questions—'Did you conduct a prior investigation into the content of the elective lectures?' (57.06% answered 'yes') and 'Did the content of the lecture you chose differ from your expectations?' (73.39% answered 'yes')—we infer that the majority of students display scant interest in performing exhaustive research on their selected lectures prior to the class. Given the advanced specialization of the course, students often struggle to predict whether a course will align with their learning objectives, armed with only limited information and basic internet searches. In fact, a substantial number of students remain uncertain about their expectations of the course, given their relative unfamiliarity with philosophy. Hence, when interpreting the aforementioned issue, we must caution against simplistic evaluations of this phe-nomenon. Nevertheless, we do not negate the possible misuse of negative freedom by students, which would bechallenging to quantify.

Furthermore, during the teaching process, we have discerned several anomalies, suggesting potential countermeasures within the classroom to curb the misuse of negative freedom. Notably, in Group A's Rounds 2, 3, and 4—which demonstrated relatively low voting rates (38.33%, 36.67%, 29.44%, respectively)—the standard deviations were also lower (17.94, 12.42, 14.66, respectively), indicating a more concentrated voting pattern when participation rates were diminished. These three rounds of lectures exhibited an evident continuity, with the instructor drawing attention to the logical links between current, preceding, and subsequent content. Students were advised that should they find this continuous content appealing, they would need to opt for it via voting. We posit that attentive and engaged students represent the relative elite of the classroom, and we have noted that the choices of these elite students tend to be more consolidated and frequently align with the instructor's recommendations. If the tokenomics is in their favor, then the practice of selection may lead in a reasonable direction.

This observation contrasts with the seemingly rational decision made by students in Group B. It appears that these students are influenced more significantly by the "hidden curriculum" and may be motivated either by its inherent rational components or by the curriculum's centralizing role. However, the precise driving factor remains uncertain, warranting further research in the future.

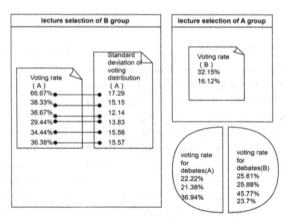

Fig. 2 Comparative analysis of voting rate and standard deviation of voting distribution across various rounds of debates for groups A and B.

9 Conclusions

As anticipated, there were several challenges encountered in effectively implementing our pedagogical design, which melds DAO and democratic education. However, unexpectedly, students' understanding of and aspiration towards decentralization exceeded our expectations and were more positive and accurate. Given suitable external conditions, we have good reason to anticipate a rise in positive classroom behaviour. Another notable potential discovery is that within an architecturally decentralized class, an appropriate operation of tokenomics could foster a rational, positive, and autonomous enactment of classroom liberty. Furthermore, a plausible hypothesis for this scenario is related to the potential power derived from architectural decentralization, particularly as wielded by elite students. These students, due to tokenomics and reward mechanisms, could exert considerable influence within the class.

As the spectrum of DAO applications expands from micro to macro levels, our thinking should evolve correspondingly. The power of tokenomics will become more substantial and complex, thereby bringing the issue of DAO governance to the fore. Once this occurs, the novel research domain of DAOs for education warrants exploration.

Acknowledgement. This research is supported by the grand of China National Social Science Fund Youth Project in Education "Contemporary Interpretation and Operational Mechanism Research of Teacher's Sense of Responsibility" [no. CEA190265].

References

1. Zhang, L., et al.: Blockchain: application in the system of teaching informatization management of higher education. In: 3rd International Conference on Smart BlockChain (SmartBlock), pp. 185–190. IEEE. Zhengzhou, China (2020)
2. Sahu, M.: Top 9 Blockchain Applications in Education. https://www.upgrad.com/blog/blockchain-applications-in-education/. Accessed 21 June 2023

3. Baas, M., Schuwer, R., van den Berg, E., et al.: The role of brokers in cultivating an inter-institutional community around open educational resources in higher education. High. Educ. **85**, 999–1019 (2023)
4. Boss, S., Sifat, I.: Decentralized Autonomous Organizations and Corporate Agency Theory (2022). https://www.researchgate.net/publication/364821197_Decentralized_Autonomous_Organizations_and_Corporate_Agency_Theory. Accessed 21 June 2023
5. Atish Mistry, B.R., Meyer, S., Saraf, V.: Reimagining education in a decentralized world. From Web3 to Ed3 - Reimagining Education in a Decentralized World. https://ed3.mirror.xyz/0U3QG8-4K6CD_ltU6SJyKN3-uBD3x6nEFs-YeShzYmk. Accessed 21 June 2021
6. Scott Meyer, V.S.: DAO.edu - The Future of Decentralized Learning. https://ed3.mirror.xyz/VJUCPEMKKvh5Fyh6Gb1_YEZrl2FCAP6jgmsByuCCkmA. Accessed 21 June 2023
7. Morrison, K.A.: Democratic classrooms: promises and challenges of student voice and choice, part one. Educ. Horizons **87**(1), 50–60 (2008)
8. Buterin, V.: The Meaning of Decentralization. https://medium.com/@VitalikButerin/the-meaning-of-decentralization-a0c92b76a274. Accessed 21 June 2023
9. Rouf, K.: Moving towards democratic classrooms for the students at the University of Toronto. Int. J. Res. Stud. Educ. Technol. **1**(2), 3–15 (2012)
10. Freire, P.: Pedagogy of the oppressed. Bloomsbury publishing USA (2018)
11. Shor, I.: When students have power: Negotiating authority in a critical pedagogy. University of Chicago Press (2014)

A Blockchain-Based Micro-services Architecture for Distributed Business

Sheng He[1,2](✉) [iD], Yishuang Ning[1,2], Dengbin Xiong[1,2], and Junhui Ma[1,2]

[1] National Engineering Research Center for Supporting Software of Enterprise Internet Services, Shenzhen 518057, China
[2] Kingdee Research, Kingdee International Software Group, Shenzhen 518057, China
heshengpku@gmail.com

Abstract. With the growth of modern businesses in scale and complexity, digital applications that span service boundaries, connect multiple organizations, and manage user identities require careful consideration. Existing enterprise architectures are monolithic, creating obstacles for digital transformation to distributed multi-enterprise ecosystems. We propose a blockchain-based micro-services architecture that enables the self-driven construction of distributed businesses with capabilities for adaptation, innovation, and robustness. By extending the concepts of Service Oriented Architecture (SOA) and Enterprise Service Bus (ESB), we developed the Blockchain Service Bus (BSB) model across enterprise scenarios. Different entities can register micro-services on the blockchain to form a unified, standardized platform that accelerates a new stage of the distributed ecosystem. Under this architecture, end-users can own a unified, decentralized identity. It allows the seamless integration of services across organizations in a federated economy, motivating scalable collaborative business models.

Keywords: Blockchain Service Bus · Micro-services Architecture · Distributed Business · Federated Economy · Privacy-preserving

1 Introduction

As modern businesses grow increasingly large and complex, enterprises are recognizing the unique benefits of distributed ecosystems [1]. With advancements in blockchain technology [2] enabling Web3 and the Metaverse [3,4], blockchain protocols are believed to become a foundational infrastructure for the next generation of decentralized business models [5]. New technologies like consensus algorithms [6,7], smart contracts [8,9], cryptography [10], secure multi-party computing [11], federated learning [12], and decentralized identity introduce both opportunities and challenges for traditional business architectures to adapt the distributed and decentralized business models [13]. To meet the demands of distributed business and new economic paradigms built on this infrastructure, enterprises require a new computing paradigm.

Q. Wang et al. (Eds.): ICBC 2023, LNCS 14206, pp. 38–53, 2023.
https://doi.org/10.1007/978-3-031-44920-8_3

While most enterprises have adopted micro-services architectures [14], their business and IT systems remain tightly coupled. Micro-services architecture, a modern variant of Service-Oriented Architecture (SOA) [15], emphasizes and structures applications as loosely coupled services. Concepts like Enterprise Service Bus (ESB) [16] promote lightweight protocols and fine-grained service management, enabling rapid and large-scale enterprise software growth and reducing communication complexity between internal services. However, self-aggregation and customization between micro-services cannot satisfy the standards, efficiency, and especially trust required for scenarios across multiple enterprises with a distributed infrastructure. Digital applications that span service boundaries, connect multiple organizations, and manage user identities require careful consideration.

Monolithic enterprise architectures [17] have struggled to meet increasing complexity in cross-organizational collaboration and personalized end-user requirements. We propose a blockchain-based micro-services architecture for distributed business that extends ESB to the scenarios across multiple enterprises. Our Blockchain Service Bus (BSB) model [7] enables the development of micro-services through multi-party cooperation on blockchain infrastructure. While inheriting SOA and ESB's loose coupling, reusability, and service autonomy, this architecture combined with blockchain and micro-services enables greater decentralization, security, and scalability. As distributed ledger technology (DLT) [18] and privacy computing [19] advance, cross-enterprise technologies will form unified platforms accelerating the adoption of distributed business models. We also propose a decentralized identity and access management mechanism offering end-users unified, self-owned identities across organizations. This increases security, privacy, and usability over traditional approaches.

This paper is structured as follows. Section 2 introduces the common characteristics of distributed technologies and business models, specifically the original requirements and challenges of enterprise IT architectures in distributed ecosystems. Section 3 presents our Blockchain Service Bus (BSB) model, which extends ESB and SOA concepts to create a trustable, decentralized infrastructure enabling micro-services integration across enterprises. Section 4 discusses our blockchain-based micro-services architecture and decentralized identity/access control model for end-users. It also shows how different emerging technologies interact and integrate to form a new distributed infrastructure. Section 5 demonstrates our architecture's application through a proof-of-concept prototype for distributed business. It considers effects on both enterprises and end-users. Section 6 overviews potential future distributed business scenarios where enterprises can benefit. Section 7 summarizes the paper and suggests some milestones for future research.

2 Future Is Coming of Distributed Business

Blockchain [20], Artificial Intelligence (AI) [21], the Internet of Things (IoT) [22], and other emerging technologies are enabling an era of interconnectivity between everything and everyone. In contrast with the single and tightly coupled architectures that enterprises relied on for decades, this new era demands the integration of internal enterprise services and ecosystem services into broader distributed architectures.

In this paper, "distributed" refers not just to traditional distributed systems or algorithms in the technical sense but to virtual cross-organizational interconnectivity and collaboration at a higher scope. Within distributed ecosystems, enterprises are no longer viewed as individual entities but as integral parts of an innovation network enabled by emerging technologies and business models.

2.1   Distributed Computing: The Rise of Distributed Cloud

The distributed cloud [23,24] incorporates physical locations into the definition of cloud computing and services. Within distributed clouds, enterprises can leverage compute and storage resources across geographically dispersed data centers based on regional regulations, customer locations, and cost. However, distributed cloud architectures must ensure consistent infrastructure, platform, and software services across locations. They must also guarantee high bandwidth, low latency connectivity between data centers and customers to function effectively as a unified whole.

For distributed computing, the network itself becomes the computer. Software platforms distribute computational workloads across connected machines, harnessing their collective processing power, memory, and storage. Advantages of distributed computing include:

- **Scalability**: Computing resources can be added incrementally to meet increasing demands. As new network nodes come online, the total processing power, storage, and memory rise accordingly.
- **Reliability**: The distributed nature of computing and storage reduces dependency on individual network nodes. If one node fails, its workload can be redistributed to others, leading to fault-tolerant systems.
- **Modularity**: Distributing computing across a network of standard, replaceable machines enables flexible resource allocation. Nodes can be added or replaced easily as business needs change.

However, distributed computing also introduces challenges including:

- **Complexity**: Managing hardware and software upgrades, configurations, and maintenance across a network of computing nodes adds layers of complexity.
- **Security**: Widely distributing computing power and data storage across networks also expands the attack surface, requiring robust identity, access control and threat monitoring solutions.
- **Network Reliance**: Unreliable or insufficient network bandwidth and latency directly impact performance, reliability, and security.
- **Governance**: Policy definition/enforcement, resource/cost allocation, and management/monitoring of distributed computing resources require a unified approach.

With blockchain, software-defined networking (SDN) [25], federated learning and secure multi-party computing (SMPC), distributed computing can transform enterprises into modular, reliable, and secure collaborative networks.

2.2 Distributed Storage: Delicate Balance for Critical Needs

For enterprise applications, distributed storage solutions must balance critical needs like data security, privacy, and governance. Distributed storage spreads data across geographically separate servers, protecting against localized failures and attacks. Distributed storage offers several advantages including:

- **Durability**: By storing data across multiple physical servers and locations, the failure of any single node does not result in data loss.
- **Scalability**: Adding more storage nodes increases total storage capacity linearly. Distributed storage solutions can scale quickly to meet enterprise demands.
- **Availability**: If one node or internet data center (IDC) goes down, data remains available through other locations, ensuring high overall availability.

However, distributing privacy data or encrypted data with consistent access controls across locations poses challenges. Enterprises must find solutions that provide the resilience and scalability of distributed storage while also meeting stringent data protection requirements. It also introduces difficulties such as:

- **Data Security**: Distributing data and access controls consistently across storage locations is complex. Ensuring only authorized users can access data wherever it resides is challenging.
- **Privacy Regulation**: Laws like GDPR [26] require controlled privacy data use and storage. Distributed storage must have strong governance preventing unauthorized data access, transfer, and processing regardless of data location.
- **Management**: Provisioning, configuring, monitoring, upgrading, and maintaining distributed storage nodes and software systems across locations demands a unified approach to management at global scale.
- **Network Constraints**: Distributing storage across IDCs relies heavily on network connectivity between locations.

Most enterprise data storage solutions remain centralized, relying on cloud services prone to single points of failure like service disruptions, privacy leaks, censorship, and unclear data ownership. Blockchain enables distributed and permanent data storage, combining storage and computing in one system - a capability poised to shape future applications. For structured data, blockchains like Ethereum [27] distribute the storage of transaction records and application states but cannot scale to large volumes alone. Layer 2 solutions built on blockchains [28] facilitate structured data storage via sidechains or off-chain storage with on-chain hashes. Protocols like the InterPlanetary File System (IPFS) [29] create distributed networks where nodes store file fragments, linked into complete files via content addressing. However, implementing enterprise requirements like access control, encryption, and node incentivation on IPFS remains challenging.

Distributed storage models of the future will rely on breakthroughs in crypto-graphic techniques tailored to a decentralized paradigm where information flows securely across boundaries. Mature privacy-enhancing computation integrated with distributed storage systems and networks could hold the key to distributed business models of the future.

2.3   Distributed Business: Common Attributes and Technological Challenges

Distributed businesses share common attributes like service modularity, virtual organizational structures, and collaborative ecosystems. Services maintained by ecosystem partners vs. a central provider lead to greater customization and cus-tomer responsiveness.

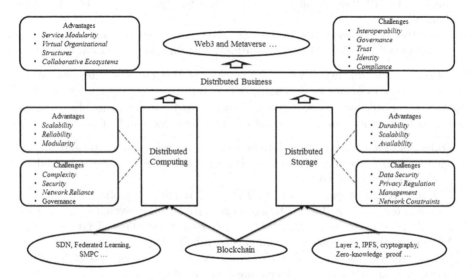

Fig. 1. The advantage analysis and technological challenges of distributed business which supported by distributed computing and distributed storage

- **Service Modularity**: Distributed businesses break down processes and offer-ings into modular components driven by events, accessed through APIs, and delivered by separate and loosely connected subsystems.
- **Virtual Organizational Structures**: Distributed businesses are virtual organizations where ownership, resources, and control are distributed across ecosystem participants rather than held within a traditional company hierar-chy.
- **Collaborative Ecosystems**: Distributed businesses develop as collaborative ecosystems of partners contributing data, services, and platforms to co-create value in a secure and compliant way.

The distributed and collaborative nature of these new business models demands rethinking value creation, e.g. from linear supply chains to networked co-production and open-source development. However, it also demands strong interoperability and governance frameworks, even facing ethical problems [30]. Without them, distributed businesses struggle to coordinate modularized services and scale solutions into mainstream commercialization. The technological challenges include:

- **Interoperability**: Without interoperability, distributed businesses cannot fully realize collaborative advantages as data/service silos persist and a fragmented user experience undermines adoption.
- **Governance**: Inadequate governance in distributed decision-making has risks around forking, fractured compliance requirements, and uncoordinated responses to issues management or market change.
- **Trust**: Establishing trusted digital relationships and transactions between ecosystem participants without traditional hierarchical controls relies on cryptographic techniques to verify identities, enforce access controls, and protect data confidentiality. If users cannot trust distributed business services and relationships, they will not adopt them at scale.
- **Identity**: Managing end-user identities and access controls across organizational boundaries while preserving privacy demands user-centric identity schemes putting individuals in control of their personal data. Centralized or provider-owned identity undermines user trust and distributed ecosystems' virtual organizational boundaries.
- **Compliance**: Compliance must provide distributed business operators and regulators with verifiable policy conformance and auditable records to legitimize new organizational forms. Without compliance, distributed businesses cannot expand from niches to mainstream commercially.

As structured in Fig. 1, distributed business could mine value at scale. Overcoming their challenges means not only advancing technologies, frameworks, cryptography, but also new compliance, governance, and identity models purpose-built for distributed trust, virtual organizations, and cross-ecosystem interoperability. Their open, user-centric, and policy-transparent foundation can transform data, services, and relationships into self-governing digital networks with security, privacy protection, and regulatory accountability.

3   Model of Blockchain Service Bus

To achieve mainstream adoption, distributed businesses need scalable architectures for trusted and compliant cross-organization micro-services integration. The Blockchain Service Bus (BSB) model [7] extends traditional ESB architectures to serve as a decentralized and policy-enforced message bus enabling micro-services integration across enterprises.

3.1   Limitations of Traditional ESB for Distributed Business

Enterprise Service Bus (ESB) [16] and Service-Oriented Architecture (SOA) [15] models cannot inherently satisfy distributed business requirements. Their centralized governance and policy enforcement architectures were designed for the integration of systems and applications within organizational boundaries.

Reliance on ESB agents to validate trust, ensure compliance and monitor service levels between distributed partners introduces complexity and risks. Their opaque and centralized policy administration frameworks cannot provide the transparency or accountability to support regulatory conformance across enterprise boundaries. Performance bottlenecks also arise from routing all interactions through a single orchestrating platform.

While beneficial within traditional organizations, ESB architectures lack critical capabilities for governance, privacy, identity, and trust across enterprises. Extending their concepts to distributed contexts demands decentralizing policy and administration frameworks to enable transparent and compliant process integration. By decentralizing communication buses and policy governance, cross-enterprise micro-services integration can be achieved in a secure, scalable, and accountable way.

3.2   BSB Model and Its Components

BSB model extends ESB architectures with distributed trust and policy enforcement frameworks to enable cross-enterprise micro-services integration. BSB combines a message bus with blockchain-based governance via smart contracts for a scalable and compliant communication layer across enterprises.

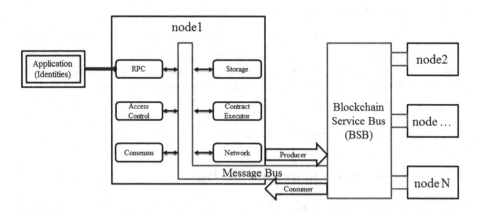

Fig. 2. Blockchain Service Bus model and its connections between the components

As Fig. 2 shown, BSB messaging channels transport encrypted service requests, events, and their responses between distributed business partners to support modular application architectures. The BSB leverages blockchain for decentralized authentication of message producers and consumers, ensuring non-repudiation of communication transactions across the bus.

As an important and distinctive component, smart contract or namely distributed application (DApp) on the blockchain establishes govenable frameworks for BSB, codifying policies and business processes to be transparently applied and audited across enterprises. Compliance-as-a-service models provide monitoring and reporting on policy conformance of smart contracts for regulatory accountability. Encryption and zero-knowledge proofs enable policy enforcement with privacy preservation.

The BSB model addresses key issues in applying advanced ESB and SOA architectures across organizational boundaries:

- **Governance and Compliance**: Smart contracts enforce customizable policies/processes with transparency and non-repudiation across BSB participants.
- **Trust and Identity**: Blockchain decentralized authentication and transaction security enable trusted information exchanges between virtual organizations.
- **Data Privacy**: Encrypted messaging channels and zero-knowledge proofs allow policy validation without exposing sensitive data.

Existing architectures cannot satisfy the demands of increasingly complex cross-organizational software ecosystems. By extending the mission of service integration to external partners, BSB unlocks network effects between ecosystems that generate value far surpassing what any single organization could achieve alone.

BSB's decentralized governance and policy frameworks are tailored to distributed business ecosystems. They support the large-scale deployment of virtual organizational structures and modular service architectures. BSB also supports compliance oracles and auditable smart contracts that demonstrate regulatory compliance, enabling new collaborative business models. By extending traditional integration architectures to distributed contexts using blockchain technology, BSB enables transparent policy enforcement, authenticated communication, and compliant micro-services integration across organizations. With on-chain governance policies defined in smart contracts and decentralized identity providing authenticated communication, BSB seamlessly and securely connects services across enterprises.

Overall, by evolving existing architectures to distributed multi-party contexts, BSB provides the standards, security and compliance to accelerate innovation across value chains responsibly and verifiably. BSB establishes an open trusted foundation for architectures to interoperate within decentralized ecosystems.

4 Blockchain-Based Micro-services Architecture

BSB model enables trusted and compliant micro-services integration between distributed business partners. However, realizing its potential at scale requires purpose-built architectures for cross-enterprise ecosystems.

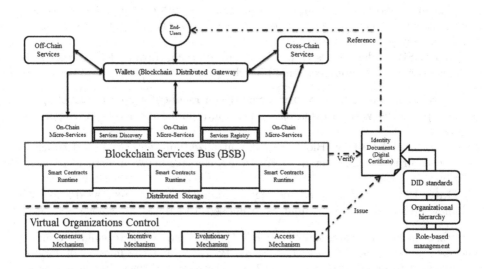

Fig. 3. Blockchain-based Micro-services Architecture

Micro-services architecture is a distributed architectural style that structures an application as a collection of loosely coupled services, enabling the continuous deployment of large and complex applications. As Fig. 3 shows, this section proposes a blockchain-native micro-services architecture and self-sovereign identity model aligned with distributed business requirements for privacy, security, and governance across organizational boundaries. Combining the BSB model with decentralized identity and micro-services management frameworks proves how collaborative ecosystems can achieve secure and regulated data sharing.

4.1 Blockchain-Native Micro-service

Micro-service architectures align with distributed business ecosystems through their modularity, decentralization, and API-enabled integration. Introducing BSB as the service discovery and registry, blockchain-native micro-services further these attributes with:

– Identified data: Each transaction is linked to immutable records on the blockchain through decentralized identifiers.
– Containers and APIs: Enabling service modularity and portability across environments/chains.

- Event-driven design: Allowing reactive and real-time logic across micro-services.
- Distributed storage: A decentralized, content-addressed, and scalable data layer.

Integrating smart contracts and incentive mechanism (e.g. tokenization), micro-services create new value streams and governable models for distributed businesses and end-users. For example, the process of data exchange can be actived by crowdsensing public data or rewarding end-users for personal data contributions.

This architecture maximizes the benefits of micro-services for distributed and decentralized contexts at the enterprise scale. Its modular and event-driven design allows rapid reconfiguration to optimize service provisioning within and across virtual organizations. Combined with the BSB model, it provides a platform for compliant process integration and value co-creation between ecosystem partners.

4.2   Decentralized Identity and Access Control

Traditional identity (ID) and access control systems lack capabilities for privacy-preserving authentication since they are designed for the internal security of enterprises. With user-centric authentication and authorization across organizational boundaries, User-centric identity gives individuals ownership and control over their personal data, credentials, and privacy. But ID systems centered on enterprise-administered accounts and access policies provide little support for user consent, data transparency, or cross-domain interoperability.

A self-sovereign identity model addresses these limitations:

- Based on standards (eg. decentralized identity, verifiable credentials): For interoperability across blockchains/networks.
- End-user control of identity data and access permissions: Both granted and revoked without third-party reliance.
- Supports authentication, authorization, and auditing with preserving privacy.

As Fig. 3 shows, decentralized identities (DIDs) are issued as identity documents through virtual organizations. End-users can hold and manage their own DIDs. When end-users access blockchain-native micro-services, BSB will control and verify data validity and security based on interactive policy, organizational hierarchy and role management.

This model gives individuals ownership of their identities to control personal data access and sharing within digital ecosystems. Policy transparency and compliance are achieved through the verifiable and auditable nature of blockchain-based credentials for DID model. Combining self-sovereign identity with blockchain-native micro-services proves how privacy-enhancing technologies enable secure and user-centric digital experiences. DID model allows seamless yet regulated data sharing and service access across distributed business ecosystems and virtual organizations.

4.3   Integration of Emerging Technologies

Realizing seamless data sharing across enterprises demands integrating solutions for identity, micro-services, messaging, and storage with blockchain frameworks. Several emerging technologies provide building blocks for a secure, compliant, and user-centric distributed infrastructure:

- Containers enable micro-service modularity and portability across environments. It also provides orchestration for automating deployment, scaling, and management of containerized applications and services.
- The distributed storage like IPFS delivers decentralized storage and content delivery. Its peer-to-peer network reduces reliance on centralized cloud storage providers.
- Blockchain technology allows the establishment of shared governance and policy frameworks through smart contracts between virtual organizations. New cross-chain networks or services maximize interoperability across existing blockchains and other distributed ledger platforms.
- Event streaming platforms enable real-time messaging, data analytics, and automation across different technologies. Event-driven architectures are optimized for reactive logic in distributed contexts.
- Hardware security modules (HSMs) provide trust anchors for securing sensitive data, transactions, and encryption keys within the distributed infrastructure.

In the Table 1, we assessed the technical maturity and the importance to data security for several blockchain-related emerging technologies as a reference. Blockchain-based micro-services architecture is a modular and adaptable technical architecture that enables the integration of related technologies.

Integration of these emerging technologies unlocks new capabilities for secure and compliant value co-creation between digital service providers and end-users. The interoperable and decentralized nature maximizes innovation across ecosystems and virtual organizations.

Table 1. A list of blockchain-related emerging technologies

Emerging technologies	Lechnical maturity	Importance to data security
Decentralized Identifiers (DIDs)	Low	High
Zero-Knowledge Proofs	Low	High
Decentralized Finance (DeFi)	Low	High
Hardware security modules (HSMs)	High	High
Containers	High	Medium
Interoperability Solutions	Low	Medium
InterPlanetary File System (IPFS)	Medium	Medium
Smart Contracts	Medium	Medium
Decentralized Applications (DApps)	Medium	Medium
Non-Fungible Tokens (NFTs)	Medium	Low
Event streaming platforms	Medium	Low

5 Use Case in Enterprise Information Architecture

The proposed blockchain-based micro-services architecture shows promise for distributed business ecosystems and federated economies. As a use case, we analyze how this architecture can be applied to optimize supply chain management (SCM).

SCM requires securely integrating data and processes across a decentralized network of suppliers, manufacturers, distributors, retailers, and customers. Traditionally, enterprise information architecture (EIA) is built around centralized platforms, resulting in data silos, single points of failure, security risks, and performance issues in large networks. Blockchain-based micro-services architecture can address these issues by implementing a peer-to-peer network. It enables a next-generation EIA leveraging the BSB model for governed, compliant data sharing and process integration.

- **Service governance**: Each organization can develop and deploy micro-services on the permissioned blockchain to represent key business capabilities such as inventory tracking, purchase ordering, logistics scheduling, and payments processing. These decentralized micro-services can then be composed into cross-organizational business processes through smart contracts and a blockchain gateway. For example, when a retailer's inventory level falls below a specified threshold, a smart contract can automatically trigger purchase orders to distributors and manufacturers, schedule deliveries, and process payments, in a transparent and auditable manner across the blockchain network.
- **Service integration**: The event-driven and service-oriented architecture enables reactive and real-time processing across micro-services. Consortium members gain a shared and immutable record of all supply chain events and transactions on the blockchain. Meanwhile, smart contracts serve as decentralized business protocols that span multiple enterprises to automate cross-organizational workflows. This includes establishing the blockchain network, onboarding new suppliers, tracing materials provenance and supply chain provenance, and managing trade finance through smart contracts. The auditability provided by the blockchain builds trust and accountability across the ecosystem.
- **Data sharing**: For data security and privacy preservation, the BSB model implements several key mechanisms. The BSB can encrypt all messages exchanged between micro-services to protect data confidentiality. Micro-services can establish data usage policies in a privacy-preserving fashion using zero-knowledge proofs before routing data access and sharing requests between them. Each network member, whether customer, supplier, or administrator, is assigned a DID to manage access control in a user-centric way.

This architecture provides a next-generation foundation for integrating distributed supply chain ecosystems. By providing shared data visibility, workflow automation, interoperability and compliance mechanisms across organizational boundaries, it enables highly adaptive, innovative and robust collaborative models for maximizing value. Rather than optimize individual processes, this architecture takes a system-level approach to power open collaboration and secure coordination of data, resources, and strategies across a complex network. By enabling seamless yet governed data sharing and exchange, it allows multiple organizations to work as an integrated whole to optimize resource planning, accelerate shared innovation, and strengthen supply chain resilience overall through strategic co-evolution. This represents the potential for blockchain-based micro-services to drive the emergence of integrated distributed ecosystems and networks in a data-oriented digital economy.

6   Scenarios and Benefits of Distributed Business

This section explores scenarios where enterprises may benefit from privacy-preserving information exchange and regulated transactions across industry consortia, alliances, and ecosystems through open frameworks for governance.

BSB model and blockchain-based micro-services architecture may present opportunities to achieve competitive advantage through innovative partnership models. Some potential scenarios for enterprises include:

- *Data Marketplaces*: It may allow enterprises to collaboratively and compliantly share data assets. Micro-services can enable the valuation, exchange, and monetization of datasets through application programming interfaces. Smart contracts could codify governance frameworks to incentivize data sharing while safeguarding privacy. Through these marketplaces, enterprises may be able to access new data streams to glean insights without the need to develop and sustain their own data repositories.
- *Collaborative Service Innovations*: Cross-industry groups jointly develop new digital services to unlock shared value where standalone services would fail. The BSB connects micro-services from different partners, smart contracts align incentives and policies, and a DID solution provides end-users a unified experience across the collaborative service.
- *Regulated Industrial Platforms*: Enterprises in highly regulated industries such as healthcare and finance could establish blockchain-based platforms to enable secure information sharing and transaction processing solely between licensed network participants. For instance, a healthcare consortium may share patient data to improve health outcomes while employing smart contracts to satisfy compliance requirements. Micro-services could furnish functionality such as claims processing with auditable event streams.
- *Ecosystem Coordination*: The BSB model may facilitate the automation of business processes across complex ecosystems where centralized market operators prove inefficient or infeasible. DIDs could provide end-users a single point of access while smart contracts establish rules governing asset usage as well as revenue and cost sharing. Ecosystem participants may gain streamlined interactions and value creation across a distributed network of partners, suppliers, and end-users.

These scenarios indicate that blockchain, micro-services, and DID solutions could enable new decentralized partnership models between enterprises by facilitating policy-enforced data and service collaboration across federated platforms. The BSB model provides a critical bridging layer for trusted and compliant transactions to overcome interoperability barriers across fragmented ecosystems where centralized control proves inefficient.

7 Summary and Conclusion

This paper has proposed a blockchain-based micro-services architecture and blockchain service bus (BSB) model to facilitate distributed business processes and federated economic interactions at scale. With distributed ledgers, decentralized identity (DID), and event-driven design, the proposed solutions aim to construct an infrastructure to enable compliant information exchange and seamless customer experiences both within and across industries. To optimize operations and enhance ecological value, the proposed solutions demonstrate how digital platforms could support partnership models across organizational boundaries.

Realizing this architecture requires progress across multiple dimensions like standards and platform development. For enterprises, integrating blockchain needs new tools and skills. Open standards are required to enable interoperability between data, identity, payments, and services. Decentralized technologies need to offer security, reliability, and performance suitable for enterprises to handle workloads within collaborative environments.

Future research could explore how emerging technologies may enable new forms of value creation across distributed ecosystems. For example, analyzing how policy standards for data usage and privacy could align between jurisdictions could enable cross-border alliances built on blockchain infrastructure. In addition, studying how decentralized autonomous organizations (DAOs) might automate compliance, incentives, and revenue sharing represents an opportunity to enhance trust within future environments like the Metaverse. Finally, examining how technologies such as AI and IoT could integrate with and enhance blockchain architectures may reveal new prospects for automation, analytics, and functionality across organizations. As businesses become more globally interconnected, blockchain may emerge as a critical medium through which enterprises can access shared data, gain actionable insights, and better serve customers across distributed platforms and partnerships.

Acknowledgement. This work is supported by the Key-Area R&D Program of Guangdong Province, China (Grant No. 2020B0101090003) and General Program of Shenzhen Science and Technology Plan, China (Grant No. JSGG20191129110603831). The authors would like to express our sincere gratitude to Dr. Liang-Jie Zhang, Dr. Huan Chen and Dr. Jing Zeng for their insightful discussions and invaluable assistance.

References

1. Senyo, P.K., Liu, K., Effah, J.: Digital business ecosystem: literature review and a framework for future research. Int. J. Inf. Manage. **47**, 52–64 (2019). https://doi.org/10.1016/j.ijinfomgt.2019.01.002

2. Zhang, LJ. et al.: BCOA: blockchain open architecture. In: Xu, C., Xia, Y., Zhang, Y., Zhang, LJ. (eds.) ICWS 2021. LNCS, vol. 12994, pp. 90–111. Springer, Cham. (2022). https://doi.org/10.1007/978-3-030-96140-4_7

3. Zhang, LJ.: MRA: metaverse reference architecture. In: Tekinerdogan, B., Wang, Y., Zhang, L.J. (eds.) ICIOT 2021. LNCS, vol. 12993, pp. 102–120. Springer, Cham. (2022). https://doi.org/10.1007/978-3-030-96068-1_8

4. Rawal, B. S. et al.: Opportunities and challenges in metaverse the rise of digital universe. In: Zhang, L.J. (eds.) Metaverse 2022. LNCS, vol. 13737, pp. 3–17. Springer, Cham. (2022). https://doi.org/10.1007/978-3-031-23518-4_1

5. He, S., Xing, C., Zhang, L.J.: A business-oriented schema for blockchain network operation. In: Chen, S., Wang, H., Zhang, LJ. (eds.) ICBC 2018. LNCS, vol. 10974, pp. 277–284. Springer, Cham. (2018). https://doi.org/10.1007/978-3-319-94478-4_21

6. Chaudhry, N., Yousaf M. M.: Consensus algorithms in blockchain: comparative analysis, challenges and opportunities. In: 2018 12th International Conference on Open Source Systems and Technologies (ICOSST), pp. 54–63. (2018). https://doi.org/10.1109/ICOSST.2018.8632190

7. He, S., et al.: Layered Consensus Mechanism in Consortium Blockchain for Enterprise Services. In: Joshi, J., Nepal, S., Zhang, Q., Zhang, L.J. (eds.) ICBC 2019. LNCS, vol. 11521, pp. 49–64. Springer, Cham. (2019). https://doi.org/10.1007/978-3-030-23404-1_4

8. Zheng, Z., et al.: An overview on smart contracts: Challenges, advances and platforms. Futur. Gener. Comput. Syst. **105**, 475–491 (2020). https://doi.org/10.1016/j.future.2019.12.019

9. Shyamasundar, R.K.: A Framework of Runtime Monitoring for Correct Execution of Smart Contracts. In: Chen, S., Shyamasundar, R.K., Zhang, LJ. (eds.) ICBC 2022. LNCS, vol. 13733, pp. 92–116. Springer, Cham. (2022). https://doi.org/10.1007/978-3-031-23495-8_7

10. Fernandez-Carames, T.M., Fraga-Lamas, P.: Towards post-quantum blockchain: a review on blockchain cryptography resistant to quantum computing attacks. IEEE access **8**, 21091–21116 (2020). https://doi.org/10.1109/ACCESS.2020.2968985

11. Zhao, C., et al.: Secure multi-party computation: theory, practice and applications. Inf. Sci. **476**, 357–372 (2019). https://doi.org/10.1016/j.ins.2018.10.024

12. Yang, Q., et al.: Federated machine learning: concept and applications. ACM Trans. Intell. Syst. Technol. **10**(2), 1–19 (2019). https://doi.org/10.1145/3298981

13. Zhang, LJ., Jeckle, M.: The next big thing: web services collaboration. In: Jeckle, M., Zhang, L.J. (eds.) Web Services-ICWS-Europe 2003. LNCS, vol. 2853, pp. 1–10. Springer, Heidelberg. (2003). https://doi.org/10.1007/978-3-540-39872-1_1

14. Dmitry, N., Manfred, S.S.: On micro-services architecture. Int. J. Open Inf. Technol. **2**(9), 24–27 (2014)

15. Zhang, L.J., Cai, H., Zhang, J.: Services Computing. Tsinghua University Press, Beijing (2007)

16. Chappell, D.A.: Enterprise service bus. O'Reilly Media, Inc. (2004)

17. Mazlami, G., Cito, J., Leitner, P.: Extraction of microservices from monolithic software architectures. In: 2017 IEEE International Conference on Web Services (ICWS), pp. 524–531. IEEE (2017). https://doi.org/10.1109/ICWS.2017.61

18. Varun, M., et al.: Decentralized authorization in web services using public blockchain. In: Lee, K., Zhang, L.J. (eds.) ICBC 2021. LNCS, vol. 12991, pp. 27–42. Springer, Cham (2022). https://doi.org/10.1007/978-3-030-96527-3_3

19. Feng, J., et al.: Privacy-preserving tucker train decomposition over blockchain-based encrypted industrial IoT data. IEEE Trans. Industr. Inf. **17**(7), 4904–4913 (2020). https://doi.org/10.1109/TII.2020.2968923

20. Chen, H., Zhang, L.J.: Fbaas: functional blockchain as a service. In Chen, S., Wang, H., Zhang, L.J. (eds.) ICBC 2018. LNCS, vol. 10974, pp. 243–250. Springer, Cham. (2018). https://doi.org/10.1007/978-3-319-94478-4_17

21. Ning, Y., et al.: A review of deep learning based speech synthesis. Appl. Sci. **9**(19), 4050 (2019). https://doi.org/10.3390/app9194050

22. Li, C., Zhang, LJ.: A blockchain based new secure multi-layer network model for internet of things. In: Proceedings of 2017 IEEE International Congress on Internet of Things (ICIOT), pp. 33–41. IEEE (2017). https://doi.org/10.1109/IEEE.ICIOT.2017.34

23. Zhang, L.J., Zhou, Q.: CCOA: cloud computing open architecture. In: Proceedings of 2009 IEEE International Conference on Web Services (ICWS), pp. 607–616. IEEE (2009). https://doi.org/10.1109/ICWS.2009.144

24. The CIO's Guide to Distributed Cloud, Gartner. https://www.gartner.com/smarterwithgartner/the-cios-guide-to-distributed-cloud. Accessed 12 Aug 2020

25. Lei, K., et al.: Measuring the consistency between data and control plane in SDN. IEEE/ACM Trans. Networking **31**(2), 511–525 (2022). https://doi.org/10.1109/TNET.2022.3193698

26. Voigt, P., Von dem Bussche, A.: The eu general data protection regulation (GDPR). A Practical Guide, 1st Ed., Cham: Springer International Publishing, 10(3152676), pp. 10–5555 (2017)

27. Wood G.: Ethereum, A secure decentralised generalised transaction ledger. Ethereum project yellow paper, pp. 1–32 (2014). https://gavwood.com/paper.pdf

28. Sguanci, C., Spatafora, R., Vergani, A.M.: Layer 2 blockchain scaling: A survey. arXiv preprint arXiv:2107.10881 (2021). https://doi.org/10.48550/arXiv.2107.10881

29. Krishnan, A.: Blockchain empowers social resistance and terrorism through decentralized autonomous organizations. J. Strat. Secur. **13**(1), 41–58. (2020). /10.5038/1944-0472.13.1.1743

30. Li, Y., Wei, W., Xu, J.: The exploration on ethical problems of educational metaverse. In Proceedings of International Conference on Metaverse (METAVERSE 2022). LNCS, vol. 13737, pp. 29–38. Springer, Cham. (2022). https://doi.org/10.1007/978-3-031-23518-4_3

SoK: X-assisted BFT Consensus Protocols

Gang Wang[1,2（✉）] and Mark Nixon[1]

[1] Emerson Automation Solutions, Austin, USA
[2] University of Connecticut, Storrs, USA
gang.wang.dr@gmail.com

Abstract. Blockchain, as an enabler of the current Internet infrastructure, has introduced a plethora of unique features, revolutionizing distributed systems and propelling us into a new era. Its core principles of decentralization, immutability, and transparency have enticed numerous applications to embrace the blockchain design philosophy and tailor diverse replicated solutions. At the heart of the blockchain lies the consensus protocols, which play a pivotal role in achieving distributed replication systems. The distributed system community has invested significant efforts in comprehensively studying the technical components of consensus to enable agreement among a group of nodes. Nonetheless, the presence of various faults and trust issues poses challenges in designing resilient systems for practical applications. To address this, Byzantine fault-tolerant (BFT) state machine replication (SMR) emerges as an ideal candidate capable of tolerating arbitrary faulty behaviors. Despite its promise, the inherent complexity and rapid evolution of BFT consensus protocols hinder their practical adaptation to different application domains. Remarkably, there exists a wealth of exceptional Byzantine-based replicated solutions and innovative ideas that have notably improved performance, availability, and resource efficiency. This paper aims to conduct a systematic and comprehensive study of X-assisted BFT consensus protocols, with a specific focus on the blockchain era. For instance, numerous studies have explored the utilization of trusted components and cryptographic primitives to assist in tolerating Byzantine nodes and reducing the number of communication rounds. We delve into the essentials of BFT consensus protocols for blockchains in Byzantine settings. We then decompose the state-of-the-art solutions to gain a comprehensive BFT consensus in detail. For each X-assisted protocol, we conduct an in-depth discussion of its essential architectural building blocks and the key techniques employed. We aim that this paper can provide system researchers and developers with a concrete view of the current design landscape and facilitate their quest for practical solutions to specific problems.

1 Introduction

The consensus protocol serves as the *core* of the blockchain, providing essential agreement services that significantly impact the performance and scalability of

Q. Wang et al. (Eds.): ICBC 2023, LNCS 14206, pp. 54–71, 2023.
https://doi.org/10.1007/978-3-031-44920-8_4

the entire system. In the absence of trusted intermediaries, participants in a blockchain network may act arbitrarily and deviate from the established consensus procedures, creating what can be described as a Byzantine environment. While blockchain can leverage various technologies for consensus, state replication, and transaction broadcasting, uncertainties in network connectivity can lead to node crashes or subversion by adversaries. To address these challenges, proof-based protocols have been developed for blockchain, such as Proof-of-Work (PoW) in Bitcoin [1]. However, these protocols often lack energy efficiency and may lead to power shortages. Fortunately, Byzantine fault-tolerant (BFT) state machine replication (SMR) offers promising opportunities to design consensus protocols that can tolerate arbitrary faults [2]. The underlying BFT SMR replicates the state of each replica in the system, rendering it capable of withstanding diverse faults and making it suitable for practical and critical applications. However, designing a functioning BFT system remains a challenging task, primarily due to its inherent complexity.

In general, a consensus protocol must satisfy three fundamental requirements [3]: (a) *Non-triviality:* If a correct entity outputs a value v, then some entity proposed v. (b) *Safety:* If a correct entity outputs a value v, then all correct entities output the same value v. (c) *Liveness:* If all correct entities initiated the protocol, then, eventually, all correct entities output some value. However, Fisher, Lynch, and Paterson (FLP) [4] demonstrated the *FLP impossibility*, proving that a deterministic agreement protocol in an asynchronous network cannot guarantee liveness if one entity may crash, even when links are assumed to be reliable. In an asynchronous system, it is impossible to distinguish between a crashed node and a correct one. Therefore, deciding the full network's state and deducing an agreed-upon output from it is deemed impossible. Nevertheless, several extensions have been developed to circumvent the FLP result and achieve asynchronous consensus. These extensions include randomization, timing assumptions, failure detectors, and strong primitives [5]. Over the course of two decades, BFT algorithms have evolved into a diverse array of protocols and applications. However, this progress has been primarily designed for closed groups based on specific application scenarios.

BFT consensus protocols form the crux of blockchain technology, determining its applicability to practical real-world scenarios. The literature encompasses numerous works discussing different aspects of Byzantine-related protocols, ranging from theoretical foundations to practical prototype deployments. While the application of BFT protocols to blockchain holds promise, it also faces significant design challenges when considering the specific requirements of the blockchain environment. In the literature, some works have explored the integration of BFT consensus protocols into the blockchain ecosystem, such as the work [6]. This paper focuses on X-assisted BFT protocols, aiming to provide a comprehensive survey of existing X-assisted Byzantine-related protocols and in-depth discussions on their implementations. Our primary goal is to offer a concrete view of the state-of-the-art literature in the domain of Byzantine-related consensus, thereby aiding researchers and system designers in finding solutions tailored to their specific needs. For each surveyed paper, we endeavor to provide detailed information and identify potential issues when applying these protocols to blockchain scenarios. Notably, there is ample literature discussing BFT consensus protocols in general forms or from architectural and theoretical perspectives.

The rest of this paper is organized as follows. Section 2 presents well-known X-assisted BFT consensus protocols. In Sect. 3, we provide discussions and explore future directions in this domain. Finally, Sect. 4 concludes the paper (Fig. 1).

2   X-assisted BFT Protocols

X-assisted BFT consensus is primarily employed to bolster robustness or enhance scalability and efficiency. Here, the term 'X' can refer to software primitives (e.g., crypto-primitives) or hardware components (e.g., trusted hardware). The core idea behind X-assisted BFT consensus revolves around ensuring the authenticity of communicated messages. For example, certain protocols, such as SBFT [7], utilize threshold signature schemes to ensure sufficient replicas can collaboratively process requests. Similarly, protocols like Steroids [8] may leverage trusted execution environments (e.g., Intel SGX) as trusted hardware to verify message authenticity. Moreover, approaches incorporating both cryptographic primitives and trusted hardware can work in tandem to improve efficiency. For instance, FastBFT [9] integrates Trusted Execution Environments (TEEs) with a lightweight secret-sharing scheme, enabling efficient message aggregation and achieving scalable Byzantine consensus. This section provides an in-depth discussion of works on X-assisted BFT consensus protocols.

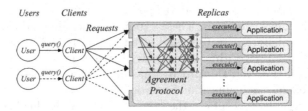

Fig. 1. Abstract of BFT replication system. Users send requests to replicas via client interfaces (with a well-defined client library). Replicas together run an agreement protocol to obtain an order on clients' requests, and then each replica executes them in its stateful application [2].

2.1   X-assisted BFT in Details

A2M. A2M, short for *Attested Append-Only Memory*, was proposed by Chun et al. in 2007 [10] to eliminate equivocation, a common source of Byzantine headaches. A2M serves as a trusted system facility that is small, easy to implement, and verifiable formally. It provides a programming abstraction of a trusted log, leading to protocol designs immune to equivocation. Equivocation refers to the ability of a faulty replica to lie in different ways to different clients or servers. The A2M protocol can be an add-on component to existing Byzantine fault-tolerant replicated state machines (e.g., PBFT, Q/U. HQ), enabling A2M-enabled protocols. In replicated state machines, the target safety guarantee is typically *linearizability*, which ensures that client requests appear to be processed in a single, totally ordered, serial schedule consistent with the order in which clients submitted their requests and received responses. A2M achieves linearizability through a small trusted log abstraction as its primitive. One key insight behind A2M is its provision of a mechanism (trusted log) that prevents participants from equivocating, thereby improving the fault-tolerance of Byzantine protocols to f out of $2f + 1$. Once an action is recorded in the log, it cannot be overwritten, as A2M does not provide a modification interface.

The overall design of A2M is based on a classic client-server system, where clients request *authenticated* operations, and the server responds to these requests. A2M's network model operates in the partially synchronous model, where a finite upper bound exists for message delivery. A2M considers two fault models: the *faulty application model*, where the node's owner is well-intentioned but unaware of the node's compromised software, and the *faulty operator model*, where the node exhibits Byzantine behavior due to malicious instructions from its owner. For each fault model, A2M has a different trusted computing base. In the first model, the service owner establishes the trusted computing base, while in the second model, the owners cannot be trusted, and a third party is responsible for setting up the trusted computing base. An A2M implementation within the trusted computing base allows a protocol to assume that a seemingly correct host can provide only a single response to each distinct protocol request. Therefore, informally, A2M can be thought of as equipping a host with a set of trusted, undeniable, ordered logs. An A2M log provides methods for *appending* values, *looking up* values within the log or obtaining the *end* of the log, as well as *truncating* and *advancing* the log suffix stored in memory. Importantly, there are no methods to replace values that have already been assigned, as A2M employs cryptography to enforce its properties and attest the log's contents to other machines. By incorporating A2M into its trusted computing base, reliable service can mitigate the effects of Byzantine faults in its untrusted components by relying on small fallback information about individual operations or histories of operations that cannot be tampered with.

TrInc. TrInc, short for *Trust Incrementer*, is a small trusted component designed to address equivocation in large-scale distributed systems, proposed by Levin et al. in 2009 [11]. TrInc is motivated by the assumption that individual components in the system are completely untrusted, necessitating the use of trusted technologies to ensure trustworthiness and eliminate equivocation. For instance, A2M uses trusted logs for this purpose. However, trusted log modules often require substantial storage space and can be challenging to implement and deploy in large distributed systems. The primary security goal of TrInc is to remove participants' ability to equivocate. It achieves this through the use of a non-decreasing trusted counter and a key, enabling it to provide a new primitive: unique, once-in-a-lifetime attestations. With this primitive, TrInc can support a broader range of protocols, including not only client-server systems but also peer-to-peer systems. One advantage of TrInc is its smaller size and simpler semantics, making it easier to deploy. It can be implemented on off-the-shelf available trusted hardware, and its core functional elements are included in a Trusted Platform Module (TPM) [12], commonly found in many modern devices. This suggests that such a component could become widely available. Additionally, TrInc utilizes a shared symmetric session key among all participants in protocol instances, significantly reducing cryptographic overhead.

One common approach to address equivocation is by using heavy-communication protocols designed to handle a threshold number of faulty participants, as exemplified by PBFT. However, TrInc aims to minimize both the communication overhead and the required number of non-faulty participants. By leveraging trusted hardware, TrInc can eliminate the ability of a malicious participant to equivocate without necessitating communication among other participants. For TrInc to be practical in distributed systems, the trusted component must be small, allowing for feasible manufacturing and deployment. It is difficult and costly to create tamper-resistant large components, making a small form factor essential. The "trinket" serves as such a trusted piece of hardware within the TrInc system. The trinket's API relies solely on its internal state, distinguishing it from typical TPMs that need to access the state of host devices (e.g., computers). Instead, the trinket requires only an untrusted channel through which it can receive input and produce output.

MinBFT. Both MinBFT and MinZyzzyva are trust-assisted BFT protocols, designed to tolerate f faulty replicas with only $2f + 1$ replicas, and were proposed by Veronese in 2011 [13]. While MinBFT is based on PBFT, MinZyzzyva is based on Zyzzyva, both being asynchronous algorithms. For the purpose of this discussion, we will focus on MinBFT, the PBFT version, to explore its technical advantages. MinBFT significantly improves efficiency compared to previous algorithms in three key metrics: the number of replicas, the simplicity of trusted services, and the number of communication steps. The main source of efficiency in MinBFT lies in the use of a simple trusted component. More precisely, the trusted services assisting in reducing the number of replicas are designed to be straightforward, facilitating verified implementations and even feasibility using commercial trusted hardware. Moreover, algorithms based on hardware tend to be simpler, approaching the level of crash fault-tolerant replication algorithms.

The successful implementation of trusted services in MinBFT is based on the usage of USIG (Unique Sequential Identifier Generator). USIG provides an interface with operations to increment the counter and verify the correct authentication of other counter values (incremented by other replicas). Each server has a local USIG service responsible for assigning unique, monotonic, and sequential identifiers to messages. Even if a server is compromised, USIG guarantees these properties, making it essential to implement the service in a tamper-proof module or a trusted component. Fortunately, the trusted component can be implemented even on commercially available trusted hardware, such as the *trusted platform module* [14].

In MinBFT, one main role of the leader is to assign a unique sequence number to each request, and this number is the counter value returned by the USIG service, ensuring the uniqueness, monotonicity, and sequentiality of identifiers. These sequence numbers remain sequential as long as the leader does not change but may change during a view change. To ensure fault-tolerance and the possibility of resending messages, servers keep a message log that stores sent messages. MinBFT employs a garbage collection mechanism based on checkpoints, similar to PBFT, to discard unnecessary messages from the log. Besides, the implementation of MinBFT and MinZyzzyva provides several levels of isolation for a trusted component used to enhance BFT algorithms. They have also implemented multiple versions of the USIG service, each using different cryptographic mechanisms. These implementations are isolated in both separate virtual machines and trusted hardware.

CheapBFT. CheapBFT is a resource-efficient BFT system based on a trusted subsystem designed to prevent equivocation, proposed by Kapitza in 2012 [15]. CheapBFT can tolerate the failure of *all but one* of the replicas that are active during normal case operation. In general, it runs a composite agreement protocol and utilizes passive replication to save resources. At a high-level perspective, the agreement protocol of CheapBFT consists of three sub-protocols: the normal case protocol *CheapTiny*, the transition protocol *CheapSwitch*, and the fall-back protocol *MinBFT*. Essentially, CheapBFT relies on an FPGA-based trusted subsystem known as *CASH* to prevent equivocation and ensure the system's integrity and correctness during the consensus process.

CASH stands for *Counter Assignment Service in Hardware*, and it is designed to assist CheapBFT with message authentication and verification. To prevent equivocation, each replica in CheapBFT must be equipped with a trusted CASH subsystem. Each CASH subsystem is initialized with a secret key and uniquely identified by a subsystem ID, corresponding to the replicas that host the subsystem. The primary function of CASH is to provide a trusted counter service, achieved by issuing message certificates for protocol messages. These certificates contain the identity *id* of the subsystem, the assigned counter value, and a MAC generated using the secret key. CASH employs symmetric-key cryptographic operations for message authentication and verification. In its basic version, CASH offers functions to create (via *createMC*) and verify (via *checkMC*) message certificates, tailored for single counter cases. For more complex scenarios with distinct counter instances and several concurrent protocols, the full version of CASH supports multiple counters, each specified by a different *counter name*. To ensure practicality, CASH is designed with two primary goals: a minimal trusted computing base and high performance. Keeping the code size of CASH small reduces the probability of program errors that could be exploited by potential attacks. Additionally, CASH ensures a high throughput during interactions involving authenticated messages to meet the system's performance requirements. Importantly, the trusted CASH subsystem is crash-fault tolerant, and its key remains secret even in the presence of Byzantine replicas (Figs. 2 and 3).

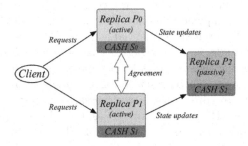

Fig. 2. CheapBFT with two active replicas and a passive replica ($f = 1$) for normal-case operation [15].

Hybster. Hybster is a hybrid BFT protocol proposed by Behl et al. in 2017 [8], which leverages a trusted subsystem for message authentication to prevent equivocation. It demonstrates the ability to tolerate up to f Byzantine faults with only $2f + 1$ replicas, thanks to the assistance of Intel SGX [16]. In modern multi-core systems, new parallelization schemes have emerged, enabling traditional BFT protocols to achieve unparalleled performance levels. Some state-of-the-art general-purpose processors offer a trusted execution environment, safeguarding software components even against the malicious behavior of an untrusted operating system. Hybster, being a highly parallelizable and formally specified hybrid SMR protocol, takes advantage of this trend. In hybrid fault models, prior SMR systems usually necessitate sequential processing of consensus instances to agree on the execution order of commands or all incoming messages. Hybster, on the other hand, explores the potential of parallelism. It abstractly presents a parallelizable structure (shown in Fig. 4), wherein multiple instances can be executed simultaneously on some physical replicas. This feature contributes to an accelerated throughput of the system. The central concept that ensures undetected

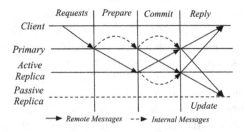

Fig. 3. CheapTiny protocol messages exchanged between a client, two active replicas, and a passive replica ($f = 1$) [15].

equivocation in Hybster involves cryptographically binding sensitive outgoing messages to a unique monotonically increasing timestamp, accomplished through the trusted subsystem. This approach enhances security while capitalizing on the benefits of parallel processing.

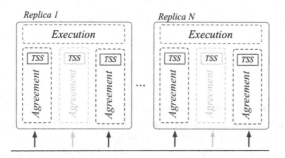

Fig. 4. Hybster: A parallelizable Hybrid [8].

In more detail, Hybster is designed around a two-phase ordering process, utilizing multiple instances of a TrInc-based trusted subsystem realized using Intel SGX to prevent equivocation. While there are other trusted schemes like A2M-PBFT and MinBFT, Hybster distinguishes itself with three key features: relaxation, formal specification, and parallelizability. Hybster relies on a trusted subsystem abstraction, known as TrInX, which is similar but not identical to TrInc [11]. It is implemented in Java and employs a consensus-oriented parallelization scheme, optimized to fully utilize multi-core CPUs. As a result, Hybster achieves high performance, and its scalability improves as the number of NIC and CPU cores increases.

FastBFT. FastBFT is a fast and scalable BFT protocol with the help of trusted hardware, proposed by Liu et al. in 2018 [9]. Essentially, FastBFT utilizes a message aggregation technique that combines a hardware-based trusted execution environment (TEE) with a lightweight secret-sharing scheme. From a high-level perspective, FastBFT also combines several other optimizations, such as optimistic execution, tree topology, and failure detection, to achieve low latency and high throughput even for large-scale networks. By using message aggregation, it can reduce the message complexity from $O(n^2)$ to $O(n)$, and the message aggregation in FastBFT does not require any public-key operations (e.g., multi-signatures), which can further reduce the computation/communication overhead. With a tree topology design in arranging nodes, FastBFT can balance computation and communication load, so that inter-server communication and message aggregation take place along the edges of the tree. Due to the optimistic design, FastBFT only requires a subset of nodes to actively run the protocol. Additionally, FastBFT utilizes a simple failure detection mechanism to handle non-primary faults efficiently.

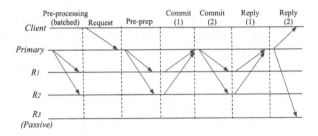

Fig. 5. Message patterns of FastBFT [9].

In general, there are two main categories for improving BFT performance when replicas rarely fail: speculative and optimistic mechanisms. The speculative mechanism typically involves not running any explicit agreement protocol (e.g., Zyzzyva). On the other hand, the optimistic mechanism only requires a subset of replicas to run the agreement protocol, while other replicas passively update their states and become actively involved only if the agreement protocol fails. The FastBFT protocol adopts an optimistic mechanism by incorporating a Trusted Execution Environment (TEE) environment. This allows replicas to remotely verify (e.g., via remote attestation) the behaviors of other replicas, with TEEs being capable of crashing but not acting in a Byzantine manner. FastBFT guarantees safety in asynchronous networks but requires weak synchrony for liveness, and each replica holds a hardware-based TEE that maintains a monotonic counter and rollback-resistant memory. The TEEs can verify one another using remote attestation and establish secure communication channels among replicas. Figure 5 illustrates the message communication pattern of the FastBFT consensus protocol. Essentially, the consensus protocol of FastBFT consists of four phases: pre-processing, request, prepare, and commit. The commit phase further includes two sub-phases that are used to update the state of replicas, similar to the execution phase in traditional BFTs. Besides, the overall FastBFT protocol also includes failure detection and view-change processes.

SACZyzzyva. SACZyzzyva, short for Single-Active Counter Zyzzyva, is a protocol designed to provide resilience to slow replicas and requiring only $3f + 1$ replicas, with just one replica needing an active monotonic counter at any given time. It was proposed by Gunn et al. in 2019 [17]. Speculative BFT protocols, such as Zyzzyva and Zyzzyva5, offer highly efficient speculative execution paths when there are no faults or delays. However, these protocols come with trade-offs. For instance, Zyzzyva requires $3f + 1$ replicas to tolerate f faults, but *even a single slow replica* can force Zyzzyva to fall back to a more expensive non-speculative operation. Similarly, while Zyzzyva5 does not necessitate a non-speculative fallback, it does require $5f + 1$ replicas to tolerate f faulty replicas. In realistic communication networks, like the Internet, which are only partially synchronous, the presence of just a single *slow* but not faulty replica can trigger non-speculative execution for each protocol run of Zyzzyva, undermining the efficiency promised by the speculative approach. SACZyzzyva addresses these drawbacks by requiring only a single replica, the primary, to have an active monotonic counter. This eliminates the need for a non-speculative fallback and enables tolerance for a subset of replicas being slow while still requiring only $3f + 1$ replicas. SACZyzzyva leverages the trusted hardware of some replicas (not all replicas) to assist in its process, following a practical setting where only some devices have the necessary hardware support. Furthermore, other BFT protocols can also adopt the single active counter approach of SACZyzzyva to reduce latency without the requirement of equipping all replicas with hardware-supported monotonic counters.

In more detail, SACZyzzyva operates under a weak-synchrony model, which allows for the analysis of liveness during a period of synchrony that will eventually occur. Additionally, SACZyzzyva assumes that *some*, but not all, replicas are equipped with a trusted component, specifically a trusted monotonic counter. The fundamental principle behind SACZyzzyva is to utilize a trusted monotonic counter in the primary replica. This counter binds a sequence of consecutive counter values to incoming requests, effectively ordering the requests without the need for communication between replicas, either directly or via the client. The primary achieves this by signing a tuple comprising the cryptographic hash of the request and a fresh counter value, resulting in a single active counter. As a result, SACZyzzyva only requires that $f + 1$ replicas have a trusted component, ensuring that there will always be at least one correct replica that can serve as the primary.

TBFT. TBFT is a TEE-based BFT protocol inspired by the structure of CFT (Crash Fault Tolerant) protocols, aiming to provide simplicity and ease of understanding. It was proposed by Zhang et al. in 2021 [18]. Unlike most existing TEE-based BFT protocols, which often involve complex operations to address security challenges introduced by TEE, TBFT takes inspiration from CFT protocols to create a straightforward and comprehensible design. In practical scenarios, many TEE-based protocols assume adversaries similar to CFT, leading to the elimination of Byzantine failures and focusing on crashed failures. The authors identified key differences between TEE-based BFT and CFT protocols and proposed four principles to bridge the gap between them. Building on these principles, TBFT introduces several improvements to enhance both performance and security. These enhancements include pipeline mechanisms, a TEE-assisted secret sharing scheme, and a trusted leader election process, all contributing to improved performance and scalability. By adopting the advantages of CFT, such as a high resilient fault rate, TBFT offers a TEE-based BFT solution with a clear and concise structure. This design approach makes TBFT more accessible for understanding and implementation compared to traditional TEE-based BFT protocols, which often tend to be more complex and challenging to grasp.

2.2 Last but Not Least

In more detail, most protocols assume that TEE may crash but will never provide malicious execution results, which makes TEE-based BFT more similar to CFT rather than BFT. However, even with the existence of TEE, a Byzantine host can still terminate TEE at any moment, schedule TEE arbitrarily, or drop, reply, delay, reorder, or modify the I/O messages of TEE. This simply can be stated that the host in TEE-based BFT may be Byzantine. Thus, it is necessary to bridge the gap between TEE-based BFT and CFT. To bridge the gap, the authors proposed four principles: *one protocol, one vote, restricted commit*, and *restricted log generation*. For one proposal, the leaders need to call a function, e.g., *create counter* for trusted monotonic counters based TEE, to assign a (c, v) (c is a monotonic counter, v is the current view) for each proposal while other replicas will keep track of the leader's (c, v).

In addition to the above-mentioned representative X-assisted BFT protocols, there are other notable works that utilize trusted hardware. Yandamuri et al. [19] proposed a scheme that utilizes small trusted hardware without increasing communication complexity, assuming the adversary controls a fraction of the network that is less than one-half. This scheme builds upon a version of HotStuff to preserve linear communication complexity while leveraging trusted hardware to tolerate a minority of corruptions. Wang et al. [20] introduced ENGRAFT, a secure enclave-guarded Raft implementation designed to achieve consensus on a cluster of $2f + 1$ replicas, with up to f replicas exhibiting Byzantine behavior (while operating within well-behaved enclaves). This solution provides an abstraction of confidential consensus, enabling privacy-preserving State Machine Replication (SMR) and facilitating the integration of a production-quality Raft implementation (BRaft). Aguilera et al. [21] proposed uBFT, a consensus protocol designed to achieve microsecond-scale latency in data centers using only $2f + 1$ replicas to tolerate up to f Byzantine failures. uBFT relies on a small, non-tailored trusted computing base and leverages disaggregated memory, ensuring a practical and bounded memory consumption. The protocol is built upon an abstraction named Consistent Tail Broadcast, which prevents equivocation while efficiently managing memory. By incorporating RDMA-based disaggregated memory, uBFT achieves an impressive end-to-end latency as low as 10 microseconds. Feng et al. [22] introduced a secure and trusted BFT (S2BFT) consensus, employing trusted committees. This protocol generates anonymous numbers using TEE for each server node and selects committees through a pseudo-random algorithm.

DAMYSUS is a streamlined protocol based on basic HotStuff, enhanced by the utilization of two fundamental trusted services: *Checker* and *Accumulator* [23]. The Checker service ensures that nodes cannot vote for conflicting blocks or misrepresent the blocks they have previously voted for, while the Accumulator service guarantees that leaders can only propose blocks consistent with past votes. The protocol requires $2f + 1$ replicas to tolerate up to f Byzantine failures and is capable of terminating within 2 communication phases. *SplitBFT* leverages TEE-based compartmentalization technology to enhance the safety and confidentiality guarantees of BFT systems, bolstering the trust in code-based deployments of permissioned blockchains [24]. Unlike traditional assumptions, *SplitBFT* acknowledges that code protected by trusted expectations may still fail. To address this, they propose to split and isolate the core logic of BFT protocols into multiple compartments. This approach improves resilience and confidentiality while simplifying the implementation of diversity. *InterTrust* is an interoperable cross-blockchain communication architecture designed to facilitate interoperability and trustworthiness among diverse blockchain systems [25]. At its core, the architecture relies on a TEE-assisted BFT consensus protocol, enabling seamless interoperability within an autonomous system. *InterTrust* incorporates two groundbreaking techniques: a threshold signature scheme and trusted hardware. The threshold signature scheme ensures consistency and verifiability in the target blockchain systems, while the trusted hardware guarantees trusted services across distinct blockchain systems. The combination of these techniques results in an efficient cross-chain communication protocol, fostering atomic swaps and facilitating interoperable operations between different blockchain systems.

3 Discussion and Future Directions

This section presents some discussion on applying BFT protocols to blockchains and explores potential future directions.

3.1 Choices on Paxos Vs. BFT

Paxos is a well-known consensus protocol that achieves agreement under crash failures [26]. Initially proposed as a solution to the FLP impossibility, Paxos can forgo progress during temporary asynchrony. However, when the system returns to synchrony, Paxos resumes its operation and ensures system consistency.

Classic Paxos (or more generally, CFT) and BFT consensus protocols explicitly model machine faults only and can be combined with orthogonal network fault models, such as the synchronous and asynchronous models. Consequently, the scope can be broadly classified into four categories [27]: synchronous CFT [28] [29], asynchronous CFT [29] [26], synchronous BFT [30] [31], and asynchronous BFT [32] [33]. Depending on the specific requirements of different blockchain applications, system designers can choose the appropriate consensus protocols from the above categories. Additionally, there exist some hybrid fault models, such as XFT [27], Byzantine Paxos [34], and heterogeneous Paxos [35], which aim to handle both CFT and BFT fault scenarios.

3.2 Hybrid Fault Models

The Byzantine fault model inherently poses difficulties in the development of consensus protocols. Typically, a BFT system may assume a powerful adversary or harsh network conditions, or even a combination of both, which introduces complexity and overhead in designing a well-replicated system [2]. As a result, some designers have observed that it may not be worthwhile to design Byzantine replicated systems for certain secure and reliable applications, such as use cases in data centers [36] [37]. Some recent works have transitioned to hybrid fault models [38] with weaker guarantees, where Byzantine replicas only account for a small portion of all faulty replicas, allowing for more practical implementations. There are several literature works that focus on these hybrid fault models, such as UpRight [39], VFT [37], and XFT [27].

Trust plays a crucial role in ensuring the effectiveness of replicated systems under hybrid·fault models. In essence, a trusted system is equipped with a small trusted computing base [40], which enables the identification of incorrectness. While a malicious replica may have the ability to operate on untrusted components, it lacks the capability to control trusted components. With the advancements in modern processors, implementing trust components in dedicated hardware modules, such as Trusted Platform Module (TPM) [41] [13], Intel's SGX [42], and ARM's TrustZone [43], to provide trusted execution environments has become more favorable. Additionally, there are software-based solutions to establish trusted components, such as via the proxy [44], a multicast ordering service [45] [46], or a virtualization layer [47] [48] [49]. In general, trusted components ensure that replicas can recover even if they become compromised [32]. They also prevent a faulty leader from successfully equivocating. As a result, whether in the form of hardware or software, trusted components offer a level of trustworthiness under hybrid fault models, helping replicated systems reach consensus with fewer required replicas. This approach proves to be more practical in certain application scenarios, such as data centers and permissioned blockchain systems.

3.3   Liveness in Consensus

A BFT consensus protocol typically achieves progress through a sequence of *views*, with each view having a designated leader responsible for driving the entire consensus process. Liveness is one of the two fundamental properties that consensus aims to achieve, along with safety. Liveness ensures that a transaction sent to all honest validators will eventually be executed. Theoretically, consensus protocols can achieve liveness by assuming an unknown *Global Stabilization Time (GST)*. After some GST period, the network may enter a period of synchrony, characterized by bounded but unknown constant message delay. However, despite claims of providing liveness guarantees, most existing works fail to offer a concrete value (e.g., latency) for this bound, making it challenging to make informed decisions.

In the literature, some works propose approaches to address liveness issues under diverse network conditions. For instance, Abraham et al. [50] introduce the concept of clock synchronization [51,52] to achieve "view synchronization," wherein each correct replica can access hardware clocks with reliable and bounded time drift. The HotStuff protocol [53] incorporates a component named *PaceMaker* to achieve view synchronization and advance progress. However, it does not provide a detailed specification of how this functionality is achieved.

Bravo et al. [54] present a similar view synchronization scheme, which provides a wrapper for BFT consensus procedures' functionality but offers formal specifications only under partial synchrony. While significant progress has been made in addressing liveness issues in BFT protocols, there is still a lack of practical live Byzantine consensus protocols that can effectively operate under fully asynchronous environments, such as the Internet. As a result, achieving a safe and live BFT consensus protocol remains a challenging task.

3.4 Scalability

Scaling protocols for BFT consensus typically prioritize either reducing the number of nodes required to tolerate f Byzantine faults [10] or minimizing the protocol's communication complexity to accommodate larger network sizes [55].

Reducing the Number of Nodes. To tolerate f Byzantine nodes that can *equivocate* in a *quorum* system like PBFT, quorums must be intersected by at least $f + 1$ nodes [56]. Consequently, if a BFT protocol requires $n = 3f + 1$ nodes, its quorum size is at least $2f + 1$. A smaller n implies lower communication costs incurred in tolerating the same number of faults. Additionally, for the same number of nodes n, the network can tolerate more faulty nodes.

Reducing Communication Complexity. Despite reducing the network size, PBFT still exhibits a communication complexity of $O(n^2)$. Byzcoin [55] proposed an optimization using the collective signing protocol (CoSi) [57], wherein the leader aggregates other nodes' messages into a single authenticated message. This approach allows each node to forward its messages to the leader and verify the aggregate message, effectively reducing the communication complexity to $O(n)$ by avoiding broadcasting. Additionally, some works [58] explore leveraging trusted execution environments (TEEs) such as Intel SGX [59] to scale distributed consensus, like the topic presented in this paper. TEEs provide protected memory and isolated execution, ensuring that regular operating systems or applications cannot control or observe the data stored or processed inside them [60]. Although trusted hardware can only crash and not act in a Byzantine manner, introducing it into consensus nodes is costly and requires specific knowledge for protocol implementation. Moreover, the security in this category can be enhanced by using cryptographic primitives, such as threshold signatures [61] [62].

Furthermore, several other intriguing research topics are emerging, such as testing technologies to evaluate the efficiency of both BFT protocols and blockchains, and schemes aimed at preventing malicious replicas' collaboration or centralization. The journey ahead for both BFT consensus protocols and blockchains remains extensive and filled with opportunities for exploration and advancement.

4   Conclusion

In recent years, research on BFT consensus has experienced a dramatic surge, partially attributed to the emergence of blockchain technology. This paper presents a Systematization of Knowledge (SoK) for existing efforts on X-assisted BFT consensus protocols. We meticulously studied the selected BFT protocols and strived to provide a comprehensive review with detailed analysis. This paper serves as a valuable starting point for exploring consensus in the realms of both X-assisted BFT and blockchain. Additionally, we present several potential research directions that can contribute to advancing reliable and robust BFT consensus within the blockchain ecosystem.

References

1. Nakamoto, S.: Bitcoin: A peer-to-peer electronic cash system. Tech. Rep, Manubot (2008)
2. Distler, T.: Byzantine fault-tolerant state-machine replication from a systems perspective. ACM Comput. Surv. (CSUR) **54**(1), 1–38 (2021)
3. Maric, O., Sprenger, C., Basin, D.: Consensus refined. In: 2015 45th Annual IEEE/IFIP International Conference on Dependable Systems and Networks, pp. 391–402. IEEE (2015)
4. Fischer, M.J., Lynch, N.A., Paterson, M.S.: Impossibility of distributed consensus with one fault process. YALE UNIV NEW HAVEN CT DEPT OF COMPUTER SCIENCE, Technical report (1982)
5. Aspnes, J.: Randomized protocols for asynchronous consensus. Distrib. Comput. **16**(2–3), 165–175 (2003)
6. Wang, G.: Sok: understanding BFT consensus in the age of blockchains. Cryptology ePrint Archive (2021)
7. Gueta, G.G., et al.: Sbft: a scalable and decentralized trust infrastructure. In: 49th Annual IEEE/IFIP International Conference on Dependable Systems and Networks (DSN), pp. 568–580. IEEE (2019)
8. Behl, J., Distler, T., Kapitza, R.: Hybrids on steroids: Sgx-based high performance bft. In: Proceedings of the Twelfth European Conference on Computer Systems, pp. 222–237 (2017)
9. Liu, J., Li, W., Karame, G.O., Asokan, N.: Scalable byzantine consensus via hardware-assisted secret sharing. IEEE Trans. Comput. **68**(1), 139–151 (2018)
10. Chun, B.-G., Maniatis, P., Shenker, S., Kubiatowicz, J.: Attested append-only memory: making adversaries stick to their word. ACM SIGOPS Operating Syst. Rev. **41**(6), 189–204 (2007)
11. Levin, D., Douceur, J.R., Lorch, J.R., Moscibroda, T.: Trinc: small trusted hardware for large distributed systems. In: NSDI, vol. 9, pp. 1–14 (2009)
12. Kinney, S.L.: Trusted platform module basics: using TPM in embedded systems. Elsevier (2006)
13. Veronese, G.S., Correia, M., Bessani, A.N., Lung, L.C., Verissimo, P.: Efficient byzantine fault-tolerance. IEEE Trans. Comput. **62**(1), 16–30 (2011)
14. Ryan, M.: Introduction to the tpm 1.2. DRAFT of March, vol. 24 (2009)
15. Kapitza, R., et al.: Cheapbft: resource-efficient byzantine fault tolerance. In: Proceedings of the 7th ACM European Conference on Computer Systems, pp. 295–308 (2012)
16. McKeen, F., et al.: Innovative instructions and software model for isolated execution. Hasp@ isca, vol. 10, no. 1 (2013)

17. Gunn, L.J., Liu, J., Vavala, B., Asokan, N.: Making speculative BFT resilient with trusted monotonic counters. In: 2019 38th Symposium on Reliable Distributed Systems (SRDS), pp. 133–13 309. IEEE (2019)
18. Zhang, J., et al.: Tbft: understandable and efficient byzantine fault tolerance using trusted execution environment. arXiv preprint arXiv:2102.01970 (2021)
19. Yandamuri, S., Abraham, I., Nayak, K., Reiter, M.K.: Communication-efficient bft using small trusted hardware to tolerate minority corruption. In: 26th International Conference on Principles of Distributed Systems (OPODIS 2022). Schloss Dagstuhl-Leibniz-Zentrum für Informatik (2023)
20. Wang, W., Deng, S., Niu, J., Reiter, M.K., Zhang, Y.: Engraft: enclave-guarded raft on byzantine faulty nodes. In: Proceedings of the 2022 ACM SIGSAC Conference on Computer and Communications Security, pp. 2841–2855 (2022)
21. Aguilera, M.K., Ben-David, N., Guerraoui, R., Murat, A., Xygkis, A., Zablotchi, I.: UBFT: microsecond-scale BFT using disaggregated memory. In: Proceedings of the 28th ACM International Conference on Architectural Support for Programming Languages and Operating Systems, vol. 2, pp. 862–877 (2023)
22. Feng, L., Ding, Y., Tan, Y., Fu, X., Wang, K., sheng Chang, J.: Trusted-committee-based secure and scalable BFT consensus for consortium blockchain. In: 2022 18th International Conference on Mobility, Sensing and Networking (MSN), pp. 363–370. IEEE (2022)
23. Decouchant, J., Kozhaya, D., Rahli, V., Yu, J.: Damysus: streamlined BFT consensus leveraging trusted components. In: Proceedings of the Seventeenth European Conference on Computer Systems, pp. 1–16 (2022)
24. Messadi, I., Becker, M.H., Bleeke, K., Jehl, L., Mokhtar, S.B., Kapitza, R.: Splitbft: improving byzantine fault tolerance safety using trusted compartments. In: Proceedings of the 23rd ACM/IFIP International Middleware Conference, pp. 56–68 (2022)
25. Wang, G., Nixon, M.: Intertrust: towards an efficient blockchain interoperability architecture with trusted services. In: 2021 IEEE International Conference on Blockchain (Blockchain), pp. 150–159. IEEE (2021)
26. Lamport, L.: The part-time parliament. ACM Trans. Comput. Syst. **16**(2), 133–169 (1998)
27. Liu, S., Viotti, P., Cachin, C., Quéma, V., Vukolić, M.: XFT: practical fault tolerance beyond crashes. In: 12th USENIX Symposium on Operating Systems Design and Implementation (OSDI 16), pp. 485–500 (2016)
28. Cristian, F., Aghili, H., Strong, R., Dolev, D.: Atomic broadcast: From simple message diffusion to byzantine agreement. Inf. Comput. **118**(1), 158–179 (1995)
29. Schneider, F.B.: Implementing fault-tolerant services using the state machine approach: a tutorial. ACM Comput. Surv. (CSUR) **22**(4), 299–319 (1990)
30. Lamport, L., Shostak, R., Pease, M.: The byzantine generals problem. ACM Trans. Program. Lang. Syst. **4**(3), 382–401 (1982)
31. Berman, P., Garay, J.A., Perry, K.J., et al.: Towards optimal distributed consensus. In: FOCS, vol. 89. Citeseer, pp. 410–415 (1989)
32. Castro, M., Liskov, B.: Practical byzantine fault tolerance and proactive recovery. ACM Transactions on Computer Systems (TOCS) **20**(4), 398–461 (2002)
33. Guerraoui, R., Knežević, N., Quéma, V., Vukolić, M.: The next 700 bft protocols. In: Proceedings of the 5th European Conference on Computer Systems, pp. 363–376 (2010)
34. Lamport, L.: Byzantizing paxos by refinement. In: International Symposium on Distributed Computing. Springer, pp. 211–224 (2011)

35. Sheff, I., Wang, X., van Renesse, R., Myers, A.C.: Heterogeneous paxos. In: 24th International Conference on Principles of Distributed Systems (OPODIS 2020). Schloss Dagstuhl-Leibniz-Zentrum für Informatik (2021)
36. Kuznetsov, P., Rodrigues, R.: Bftw3: why? when? where? workshop on the theory and practice of byzantine fault tolerance. ACM SIGACT News **40**(4), 82–86 (2010)
37. Porto, D., et al.: Visigoth fault tolerance. In: Proceedings of the Tenth European Conference on Computer Systems, pp. 1–14 (2015)
38. Thambidurai, P., Park, Y.-K.: Interactive consistency with multiple failure modes. In: Proceedings Seventh Symposium on Reliable Distributed Systems. IEEE Computer Society, pp. 93–94 (1988)
39. Clement, A.: Upright cluster services. In: Proceedings of the ACM SIGOPS 22nd Symposium on Operating Systems Principles, pp. 277–290 (2009)
40. Rushby, J.M.: Design and verification of secure systems. ACM SIGOPS Operat. Syst. Rev. **15**(5), 12–21 (1981)
41. Veronese, G.S., Correia, M., Bessani, A.N., Lung, L.C.: Ebawa: efficient byzantine agreement for wide-area networks. In: IEEE 12th International Symposium on High Assurance Systems Engineering. IEEE 2010, pp. 10–19 (2010)
42. Anati, I., Gueron, S., Johnson, S., Scarlata, V.: Innovative technology for CPU based attestation and sealing. In: Proceedings of the 2nd International Workshop on Hardware and Architectural Support for security and privacy, vol. 13, p. 7. ACM, New York (2013)
43. A. ARM: Security technology-building a secure system using trustzone technology. ARM Technical White Paper (2009)
44. Rüsch, S., Bleeke, K., Kapitza, R.: Bloxy: providing transparent and generic bft-based ordering services for blockchains. In: 2019 38th Symposium on Reliable Distributed Systems (SRDS), pp. 305–30 509. IEEE (2019)
45. Correia, M., Neves, N.F., Lung, L.C., Veríssimo, P.: Worm-it-a wormhole-based intrusion-tolerant group communication system. J. Syst. Softw. **80**(2), 178–197 (2007)
46. Correia, M., Veronese, G.S., Neves, N.F., Verissimo, P.: Byzantine consensus in asynchronous message-passing systems: a survey. Int. J. Critical Comput.-Based Syst. **2**(2), 141–161 (2011)
47. Distler, T., Popov, I., Schröder-Preikschat, W., Reiser, H.P., Kapitza, R.: Spare: replicas on hold. In: NDSS (2011)
48. Garcia, M., Bessani, A., Neves, N.: Lazarus: automatic management of diversity in bft systems. In: Proceedings of the 20th International Middleware Conference, pp. 241–254 (2019)
49. Reiser, H.P., Kapitza, R.: Hypervisor-based efficient proactive recovery. In: 26th IEEE International Symposium on Reliable Distributed Systems (SRDS 2007). IEEE 2007, pp. 83–92 (2007)
50. Abraham, I., Devadas, S., Dolev, D., Nayak, K., Ren, L.: Synchronous byzantine agreement with expected o (1) rounds, expected $o(^n2)$ communication, and optimal resilience. In: International Conference on Financial Cryptography and Data Security, pp. 320–334. Springer (2019)
51. Dolev, D., Halpern, J.Y., Simons, B., Strong, R.: Dynamic fault-tolerant clock synchronization. J. ACM (JACM) **42**(1), 143–185 (1995)
52. Simons, B.: An overview of clock synchronization. In: Fault-Tolerant Distributed Computing, pp. 84–96 (1990)
53. Yin, M., Malkhi, D., Reiter, M.K., Gueta, G.G., Abraham, I.: Hotstuff: Bft consensus with linearity and responsiveness. In: Proceedings of the 2019 ACM Symposium on Principles of Distributed Computing, pp. 347–356 (2019)

54. Bravo, M., Chockler, G., Gotsman, A.: Making byzantine consensus live. In: 34th International Symposium on Distributed Computing (DISC 2020). Schloss Dagstuhl-Leibniz-Zentrum für Informatik (2020)
55. Kogias, E.K., Jovanovic, P., Gailly, N., Khoffi, I., Gasser, L., Ford, B.: Enhancing bitcoin security and performance with strong consistency via collective signing. In: 25th usenix security symposium (usenix security 16), pp. 279–296 (2016)
56. Malkhi, D., Reiter, M.: Byzantine quorum systems. Distrib. Comput. **11**(4), 203–213 (1998)
57. Syta, E., et al.: Keeping authorities "honest or bust" with decentralized witness cosigning. In: IEEE Symposium on Security and Privacy (SP). IEEE 2016, pp. 526–545 (2016)
58. Dang, H., Dinh, A., Chang, E.-C., Ooi, B.C.: Chain of trust: can trusted hardware help scaling blockchains? arXiv preprint arXiv:1804.00399 (2018)
59. Costan, V., Devadas, S.: Intel sgx explained. IACR Cryptology ePrint Archive **2016**(086), 1–118 (2016)
60. Ekberg, J.-E., Kostiainen, K., Asokan, N.: The untapped potential of trusted execution environments on mobile devices. IEEE Secur. Privacy **12**(4), 29–37 (2014)
61. Boneh, D., Lynn, B., Shacham, H.: Short signatures from the weil pairing. In: Boyd, C. (ed.) ASIACRYPT 2001. LNCS, vol. 2248, pp. 514–532. Springer, Heidelberg (2001). https://doi.org/10.1007/3-540-45682-1_30
62. Stathakopoulous, C., Cachin, C.: Threshold signatures for blockchain systems. Swiss Federal Institute of Technology (2017)

Machine Learning and Blockchain Intersection in Cryptocurrency Price Prediction

Alireza Ashayer, Joseph Wireman[(✉)] [iD], and Nasseh Tabrizi

East Carolina University, Greenville, NC 27858, USA
wiremanj20@students.ecu.edu

Abstract. Since the introduction of Bitcoin in 2008 as the first practical decentralized cryptocurrency, the interest in cryptocurrencies and their underlying technology, Blockchain, has skyrocketed. Security, anonymity, and lack of a central controlling authority make them ideal for users who are privacy-minded. Academic research on machine learning, Blockchain, and their intersection in cryptocurrency price prediction has increased significantly in recent years. On that account, we present the review of published research that involve applications of machine learning techniques in the prediction of cryptocurrency prices. Given the novelty of Blockchain technology, the number of published research in this field is currently limited, but it is increasing rapidly. Our search resulted in a final sample of 18 papers categorized and reviewed thoroughly. Given the rising trend of research in these fields, we hope to provide a strong starting point for interested researchers.

Keywords: Blockchain · Machine learning · Cryptocurrency · Bitcoin

1 Introduction

In November 2008, Bitcoin's systematic structural specification was released by an unknown source using the pseudonym Satoshi Nakamoto [1]. Since then, despite the introduction of thousands of new cryptocurrencies, Bitcoin is still the largest and most valuable cryptocurrency in the world. At the time of writing this paper, Bitcoin has a market capitalization of more than 112 billion U.S. dollars. The combined market capitalization of all cryptocurrencies, including Bitcoin, is more than 412 billion U.S. dollars [2].

Even though there were published papers [3, 4] on similar concepts before the invention of Bitcoin, the novelty of Bitcoin and ensuing cryptocurrencies is that they solve the double-spending problem without having a central authoritative source. All transactions are stored in a distributed public ledger called Blockchain, which is computationally impractical to tamper. While initially introduced to solve the double spending problem in digital currencies, Blockchain technology has since been used for other applications fields such as databases [5] and decentralized web [6, 7].

Machine learning and its related fields have made remarkable advances in recent years [8]. Some of these technological breakthroughs have led to the creation or improvement of products that are used by billions of people worldwide [9]. Since the advent

Q. Wang et al. (Eds.): ICBC 2023, LNCS 14206, pp. 72–88, 2023.
https://doi.org/10.1007/978-3-031-44920-8_5

of machine learning and its related technologies, many researchers have focused on applying these new techniques to financial markets. Stock market prediction [10] and manipulation detection [11] are a few examples of a large body of research in this field. Cryptocurrencies are also considered to be a financial asset where, research that has been performed on financial markets can also be applied to this field.

Since the invention of Blockchain technology, most of the published research has been concentrated on non-technological aspects of Blockchain, such as legal issues and its criminal aspects [12]. Given the novelty of Blockchain technology and rapid advances in machine learning techniques, research on their union is still less mature and broader than in other research areas. Consequently, must review the existing articles in this area to help researchers better understand the current research trend and landscape.

In this research, we have reviewed and classified papers involving machine learning applications in Blockchain technology. Since cryptocurrencies were first introduced in 2008, our scope is limited to articles published between 2008 and 2022. This paper will discuss the research methodologies and results of the analysis of reviewed articles and their classifications. Furthermore, we present these studies conclusions, limitations, and implications and discuss areas that have the potential for future research.

2 Research Methodology

The motivation for this study is to understand the trend of research on cryptocurrency price prediction, with respect to machine learning, by studying and reviewing published articles. This understanding can provide other researchers and practitioners insight into the current state and future direction of research in this field. Given this motivation, we will review and verify the distribution of research papers by their year of publication, classify the study using machine learning techniques, prediction variables, and reported statistical criteria. To provide a comprehensive review of research papers, we have used the following electronic research databases:

- Science Direct
- IEEE Xplore
- ACM Digital Library
- Springer Link
- PLOS One
- arXiv
- Proquest
- Google Scholar

We performed the search on seven keywords and their mutations: "Cryptocurrency", "Bitcoin", "Ethereum", "Blockchain", "Machine learning", "Price forecasting", and "Price prediction". The abstract of each paper was reviewed next, and papers that were undoubtedly not related to Blockchain and machine learning were deleted. In case a paper's relevance could not be established with certainty by reading the abstract, or potential relevance could be discerned from the abstract, the full text of the paper was reviewed.

Since research on Blockchain is a relatively new field, the number of relevant peer-reviewed published journal papers is insufficient to limit the scope of this survey to them.

Hence, in this review paper, we widened the inclusion criteria by including journal papers, conference papers, high-quality research reports, and working papers. In this review paper, the origin of each reviewed paper is clearly marked to help the researchers decide to include or exclude them from the relevant categories.

3   Results

We selected 24 papers and classified them by year of publication, paper type, and machine learning techniques. The details and results of this classification is discussed in the following sections.

3.1 Distribution by Year

The distribution of articles between 2008 and 2022 is shown in Fig. 1. As it is apparent from the Fig. 1, the first paper that applied machine learning techniques to Blockchain technology was published [13] six years after the introduction of Blockchain as part of Bitcoin whitepaper in 2008 [1]. Since then, there has been a significant increase in the number of published papers. Over half of papers are from the last 12 months. This increase in popularity is a clear indication that a large number of researchers are now focusing their research on this relatively new field.

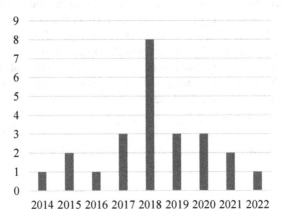

Fig. 1. Distribution of articles by year

3.2 Distribution by Type

We have included research papers of different types in our review paper to better understand the research landscape in this field. Figure 2. Shows the type of articles that we reviewed in this survey. Table 1 represents the complete list of papers and their publication type.

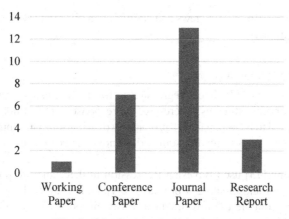

Fig. 2. Distribution of articles by type

3.3   Distribution by Machine Learning Technique

In this section, we cover machine learning techniques and algorithms that were used in papers that we have reviewed. Most of these techniques and the way they are used are covered in the following section. The complete list of papers and machine learning techniques used is presented in Table 1.

3.3.1   Linear Regression

This technique is a linear approach to modelling the relationship between a dependent variable and one or more independent variables. It works by estimating unknown model parameters from input data using linear predictor functions. Linear fit is usually calculated by minimizing the mean squared error between the predicted and actual output [14].

Authors in [14] used linear regression to investigate the predictive power of Blockchain network-based features on the future price of Bitcoin. Using this machine learning model, they were able to predict the price direction of Bitcoin, one hour in the future, with 55% accuracy.

3.3.2   Logistic Regression

Logistic Regression measures the relationship between the dependent variable and one or more independent variables. It uses a logistic function to estimate probabilities of a categorical dependent variable, unlike linear regression which is suitable for continuous variables. Logistic regression uses Maximum Likelihood Estimation to formulate the probabilities [14].

Four research reports [14, 29, 30, 45] use logistic regression to predict price fluctuations for cryptocurrencies. The authors [14] used this model to predict the price of Bitcoin one hour into the future. Other authors [29] have performed an experiment to identify the price movements of Bitcoin using Twitter sentiment analysis. The research was expanded by [30] to include data from daily news and addition of a different cryptocurrency called Ethereum, to the model.

3.3.3 Bayesian Regression

In Bayesian Regression [47], linear regression is formulated using probability distribution rather than point estimates. Therefore, the response is not estimated as a single value, but is assumed to be drawn from a probability distribution. This approach is useful when the amount of data is limited or some prior knowledge can be used in creating the model [31].

Shah and Zhang [13] used Bayesian Regression in their study to predict the price variations of Bitcoin and creating a profitable cryptocurrency trading strategy. Their strategy can nearly double the investment in a Bitcoin portfolio in less than 60 days when run against real trading data from cryptocurrency exchanges.

3.3.4 Naïve Bayes

This probabilistic classifier works by applying Bayes theorem assuming that features are independent of each other. This classifier is usually applied to text classification and sentiment analysis problems and uses maximum likelihood estimation to maximize the joint likelihood of the data [30].

Two research reports [29, 30] have used this technique for creating predictive models based on data from cryptocurrencies. In the study by [29], authors reported the possibility of identifying Bitcoin price movements based on Twitter sentiment analysis. Further research by [30], expanded on the previous study by including data from daily news headline data and adding another cryptocurrency, Ethereum, to their model.

3.3.5 Feed-Forward Artificial Neural Network

Multilayer Perceptron (MLP) is a class of feed-forward artificial neural network that has at least three layers of nodes. Each node in an MLP, except the input nodes, is a neuron that uses a nonlinear activation function to operate. The activation function defines the output of each neuron for each set of inputs and training is performed by backpropagation which is a generalization of the least mean squares algorithm.

In [18], the authors used a neural network with seven layers to improve the buy and hold trading strategy. They used technical indicators with intervals of 15 min as their input data and achieved the most favorable return by comparing four different patterns of artificial neural networks. Others including [16] utilized non-linear autoregressive with exogenous inputs MLP as their Bitcoin price forecasting model. Furthermore, they used Particle Swarm Optimization to optimize several parameters of their model which gave them the ability to accurately predict Bitcoin prices.

3.3.6 Convolutional Neural Network

Convolutional Neural Network (CNN) [32, 46] is a feed-forward artificial neural network inspired by biological processes. Hidden layers of this network typically consist of convolutional layers, among other types. Each convolutional hidden layer applies a convolutional operation to the input and then passes the result to the next layer. Even though it is mostly applied to analyzing visual imagery, some researchers have successfully used it for time series analysis.

Authors [25] present a model-less convolutional neural network that uses the price data of a set of 12 different cryptocurrencies to find the weights for a portfolio that maximizes the accumulative return in the long run. The performance of their model outperforms three different benchmarks and three other portfolio management algorithms.

3.3.7 Recurrent Neural Network

Recurrent Neural Network (RNN) is a category of artificial neural networks where connections between nodes form a directed graph along a sequence allowing the network to exhibit dynamic temporal behavior for a time sequence. Long short-term memory networks (LSTM) [33] are a special kind of RNN capable of learning long-term dependencies making them suitable for time series prediction, such as cryptocurrency price trends.

Researchers in [26] used LSTMs in order to predict Bitcoin's price movements. Their research shows that LSTMs can reach a classification accuracy of 52% in predicting the future direction of Bitcoin prices. Further research by [19] analyzed daily data for 1681 cryptocurrencies and used LSTM networks to build a predictive model for each currency which gave them the ability to devise a trading strategy that outperforms standard benchmarks. Researchers can find more details on the performance and accuracy metrics [41, 42, 44].

3.3.8 Support Vector Machine

Support Vector Machines (SVM) are non-probabilistic binary linear classifiers used in classification and regression analysis. SVMs are commonly used in text categorization, classification of images, and hand-writing recognition. In Blockchain and cryptocurrency field, a number of researchers have applied SVMs to predict Bitcoin and other cryptocurrency prices [14, 29, 30, 42, 45]. These studies have shown that other models are more accurate at predicting the Bitcoin price than SVMs.

3.3.9 Random Forest

Random Forests operate by creating many decision trees at training time and outputting either the mode of the classes or mean prediction of the individual trees. Due to their structure, compared to decision trees, random forests are less prone to overfitting to their data set. They are quick to train, require less input preparation, and provide an implicit feature selection by indicating their importance [34]. Authors [24] and [45] proposed a method to predict Bitcoin prices based on Bayesian regression and random forest learning techniques.

3.3.10   Gradient Boosting

Gradient Boosting is a technique for both regression and classification problems. It produces a prediction model that is an ensemble of weak prediction models, usually decision trees. In several studies, authors have used Gradient Boosting and related techniques, such as Extreme Gradient Boosting, to create predictive models of cryptocurrency prices [19, 22].

3.4   Prediction

Reviewed papers in this study have used different input data and various methods to forecast the future price of cryptocurrencies. As seen in Table 2, many researchers have focused on predicting the next day's closing price of one or several cryptocurrencies. A common reason for this choice is the wider availability of historic daily closing prices for these cryptocurrencies. Authors [13, 18, 25, 28] that have selected a shorter time scale for prediction are usually concerned with the performance of their models in active trading or as part of a cryptocurrency portfolio.

Nearly all the reviewed papers, with the exception of a few [22, 27], have studied Bitcoin as the only or one of the cryptocurrencies they have modeled. Bitcoin is the most popular and the most valuable cryptocurrency in terms of market cap therefore this observation is not a surprise.

To create and train their models, authors have chosen vastly different data points. While the most common one is the daily closing price time series, others [17, 22, 29, 30] have included data from other sources, such as Twitter, News, and online forums. Furthermore, some authors [15, 24] have combined data from different sources to achieve more accuracy in their prediction.

3.5   Statistical Error Criteria

To provide a better understanding of the prediction results of each study, their reported prediction statistical errors are presented in Table 3. Studies that have not provided numbers, or their metrics or are in a format that is not comparable to others, have been excluded.

Some authors have studied several cryptocurrencies, used several models, or both. In order distinguish the reported error criteria, each number is prefixed with an identifier. The first part indicates cryptocurrency. For example, BTC is short for Bitcoin and LTC is short for Litecoin. The second part indicates the models used. LR is short for Logistic Regression, BYS is short for Bayes, and so on. Please refer to Table 1 and Table 2 to find the model and cryptocurrency used for each study presented in Table 3.

In Table 3, columns represent the following statistical error criteria:

- Mean Squar Error (MSE)
- Root Mean Squar Error (RMSE)
- Mean Absolute Error (MAE)
- Mean Absolute Percentage Error (MAPE)
- Percentage of predictions that have correctly classified price movement direction (Accuracy)

One of the difficulties in comparing the reported numbers is the context in which they were calculated. In some studies, [20] authors have not normalized the prices across cryptocurrencies. Therefore, their reported results depend on the absolute price of each cryptocurrency. While in others [15, 28] the log price is used instead of the absolute price. Given this limitation, the results are still comparable with carefulness.

Based on reported error criteria of reviewed studies in Table 3, several conclusions can be reached. First, when measured by squared and absolute error criteria, logistic regression and Naïve Bayes are more accurate compared to SVMs and neural networks. On the other hand, when measured by price movement direction prediction accuracy, neural network-based models tend to perform better compared to classical statistical models with same data set and procedures.

Table 1. Papers by Machine learning Techniques

Reference	Year	Type	Machine learning techniques
H. Jang and J. Lee [15]	2018	Journal Paper	Support Vector Machines, Linear Regression, Bayesian Neural Network
N. Indera, I. Yassin, A. Zabidi and Z. Rizman [16]	2018	Journal Paper	Multilayer Perceptron, Particle Swarm Optimization
Y. B. Kim, J. G. Kim, W. Kim, J. H. Im and T. Kim [17]	2016	Journal Paper	Averaged One-dependence Estimators
M. Nakano, A. Takahashi and S. Takahashi [18]	2018	Journal Paper	Multilayer Perceptron
L. Alessandretti, A. ElBahrawy, L. M. Aiello and A. Baronchelli [19]	2018	Journal Paper	Long Short Term Memory, Extreme Gradient Boosting
A. Altan, S. Karasu and S. Bekiros [20]	2019	Journal Paper	Ensemble (Emirical Wavelength Transform, Long Short Term Memory, Cuckoo Search Optimization)
D. C. Mallqui and R. A. Fernandes [21]	2019	Journal Paper	Artificial Neural Network, Support Vector Machines, Ensemble (RNN and K-Means)
T. R. Li, A. S. Chamrajnagar, X. R. Fong, N. R. Rizik and F. Fu [22]	2018	Journal Paper	Extreme Gradient Boosting
B. Ly, D. Timaul, A. Lukanan, J. Lau and E. Steinmetz [23]	2018	Conference Paper	Deep Neural Networks
D. Shah and K. Zhang [13]	2014	Conference Paper	Bayesian Regression
S. Valenkar, S. Valecha and S. Maji [24]	2018	Conference Paper	Bayesian Regression, Random Forest

(*continued*)

Table 1. (*continued*)

Reference	Year	Type	Machine learning techniques
Z. Jiang and J. Liang [25]	2017	Conference Paper	Convolutional Neural Network
S. McNally, J. Roche and S. Caton [26]	2018	Conference Paper	Recurrent Neural Network, Long Short Term Memory
H.-M. Kim, G.-W. Bock and G. Lee [27]	2019	Conference Paper	Correlation Analysis
T. Guo and N. Antulov-Fantulin [28]	2019	Working Paper	Temporal Mixture Model
A. Greaves and B. Au [14]	2015	Research Report	Linear Regresssion, Logistic Regression, Support Vector Machines, Multilayer Perceptron
S. Colianni, S. Rosales and M. Signorotti [29]	2015	Research Report	Logistic Regression, Naïve Bayes, Support Vector Machines
C. Lamon, E. Nielsen and E. Redondo [30]	2017	Research Report	Logistic Regression, Naïve Bayes, Support Vector Machines
X. Du, Z. Tang, J. Wu, K. Chen, Y. Cai [40]	2022	Journal Paper	Autoregressive Integrated Moving Average, Backpropagation Neural Network, Support Vector Regression, Extreme Learning Machine
T. Muniye, S. Satapathy, M. Rout [41]	2021	Journal Paper	Recurrent Neural Network, Long Short Term Memory
M. Mudassir, S. Bennbaia, D. Unal, M. Hammoudeh [42]	2020	Journal paper	Long Short Term Memory, Support Vector Machines, Artificial Neural Network
Huihai Jiang [43]	2021	Conference Paper	Logistic Regression, K-Nearest Neighbors
P. Jay, V. Kalariya, P. Parmar, S. Tanwar, N. Kumar, M. Alazab [44]	2020	Journal Paper	Multi-Layer Perceptron, Long Short Term Memory
Z. Chen, Chunhong Li and Wenjun Sun [45]	2020	Journal Paper	Logistic Regression, Linear Discrimininant Analysis, Random Forest, Support Vector Machines, Long Short Term Memory

Table 2. Papers by Prediction type and predictor data

Reference	Prediction Type	Cryptocurrencies	Predictor Data
H. Jang and J. Lee [15]	1 Day Ahead	BTC	Blockchain Information, Macro-economic Indices, Global Currency Ratios
N. Indera, I. Yassin, A. Zabidi and Z. Rizman [16]	1 Day Ahead	BTC	Daily Closing Price Time Series
Y. B. Kim, J. G. Kim, W. Kim, J. H. Im and T. Kim [17]	1–13 Day Ahead	BTC, ETH, XRP	Online Forums Sentiment Analysis
M. Nakano, A. Takahashi and S. Takahashi [18]	15 min Ahead	BTC	Daily Closing Price Time Series
L. Alessandretti, A. ElBahrawy, L. M. Aiello and A. Baronchelli [19]	1 Day Ahead	1681 Cryptocurrencies	Daily Closing Price Time Series, Market Cap, Trading Volume
A. Altan, S. Karasu and S. Bekiros [20]	1 Day Ahead	BTC, XRP, DASH, LTC	Daily Closing Price Time Series
D. C. Mallqui and R. A. Fernandes [21]	1 Day Ahead	BTC	Daily Closing Price Time Series
T. R. Li, A. S. Chamrajnagar, X. R. Fong, N. R. Rizik and F. Fu [22]	1 h Ahead	ZClassic	Twitter Sentiment Analysis
B. Ly, D. Timaul, A. Lukanan, J. Lau and E. Steinmetz [23]	7 Day Ahead	BTC	Daily Closing Price Time Series
D. Shah and K. Zhang [13]	10 s Ahead	BTC	Daily Closing Price Time Series
S. Valenkar, S. Valecha and S. Maji [24]	1 Day Ahead	BTC	Blockchain Information, Daily Closing Price Time Series
Z. Jiang and J. Liang [25]	30 min Ahead	12 Cryptocurrencies	Daily Closing Price Time Series

(*continued*)

Table 2. (*continued*)

Reference	Prediction Type	Cryptocurrencies	Predictor Data
S. McNally, J. Roche and S. Caton [26]	1 Day Ahead	BTC	Daily Closing Price Time Series
H.-M. Kim, G.-W. Bock and G. Lee [27]	Same Day	ETH	Blockchain Information, Macro-economic Indices, Global Currency Ratios
T. Guo and N. Antulov-Fantulin [28]	1 h Ahead	BTC	Volatility Series, Order Book Data
A. Greaves and B. Au [14]	1 Day Ahead	BTC	Bitcoin Transaction Data
S. Colianni, S. Rosales and M. Signorotti [29]	1 Day Ahead and 1 h Ahead	BTC	Twitter Sentiment Analysis
C. Lamon, E. Nielsen and E. Redondo [30]	1 Day Ahead	BTC, LTC, ETH	News and Social Media
X. Du, Z. Tang, J. Wu, K. Chen, Y. Cai [40]	1 Day Ahead and 5 Days Ahead	BTC, ETH	Daily Closing Prices
T. Muniye, S. Satapathy, M. Rout [41]	1 Day Ahead, 3 Days Ahead, 5 Days Ahead, 7 Days Ahead and 15 Days Ahead	BTC	Opening Price, High Price, Low Price, Market Cap and Closing Price
M. Mudassir, S. Bennbaia, D. Unal, M. Hammoudeh [42]	End of Day, 1 Week Ahead and 30–90 Days Ahead	BTC	Blockchain Information, Transaction fee, Hash Rate, Total Transactions
Huihai Jiang [43]	1 Day Ahead	BTC	Blockchain Information

(*continued*)

Table 2. (*continued*)

Reference	Prediction Type	Cryptocurrencies	Predictor Data
P. Jay, V. Kalariya, P. Parmar, S. Tanwar, N. Kumar, M. Alazab [44]	1 Day Ahead	BTC, LTC, ETH	Total Transactions, Market Volume, Mining Difficulty and Hashrate, Mining Profitability, Transaction Fee, Confirmation time, Market Capitalization, Social Media, Highest and Lowest Value
Z. Chen, Chunhong Li and Wenjun Sun [45]	1 Day Ahead and 5 min ahead	BTC	Social Media, Blockchain Information, Gold Spot Price

Table 3. Papers by Reported Error

Reference	MSE	RMSE	MAE	MAPE(%)	Accuracy(%)
A. Greaves and B. Au [14]	BTC-LR: 1.94 BTC-SVM: 1.98	-	-	-	BTC-LR: 54.3 BTC-SVM: 53.7 BTC-NN: 55.1
H. Jang and J. Lee [15]	-	**(Log Price)** BTC-LR: 0.0935 BTC-BYS: 0.0069 BTC-SVM: 0.2742	-	**(Log Price)** BTC-LR: 0.0712 BTC-BYS: 0.0180 BTC-SVM: 0.0404	-
Y. B. Kim, J. G. Kim, W. Kim, J. H. Im and T. Kim [17]	-	-	-	-	**(1 Day Ahead)** BTC-AOE: 51.579 ETH-AOE: 53.739 XRP-AOE: 61.314
T. Guo and N. Antulov-Fantulin [28]	-	**(Log Price)** BTC-TM: 0.083	-	-	-

(*continued*)

Table 3. (*continued*)

Reference	MSE	RMSE	MAE	MAPE(%)	Accuracy(%)
A. Altan, S. Karasu and S. Bekiros [20]	-	BTC-ENS: 623.41 XRP-ENS: 0.0088 DASH-ENS: 2.7776 LTC-ENS: 1.7989	BTC-ENS: 500.16 XRP-ENS: 0.0064 DASH-ENS: 2.0746 LTC-ENS: 1.1066	BTC-ENS: 3.55 XRP-ENS: 1.72 DASH-ENS: 1.47 LTC-ENS: 2.77	-
D. C. Mallqui and R. A. Fernandes [21]	-	BTC-ANN: 25.84 BTC-RNN: 18.56 BTC-SVM: 15.92	BTC-ANN: 19.06 BTC-RNN: 14.56 BTC-SVM: 9.63	BTC-ANN: 3.86 BTC-RNN: 3.08 BTC-SVM: 1.91	-
S. McNally, J. Roche and S. Caton [26]	-	-	-	-	BTC-LSTM: 52.78 BTC-RNN: 50.25 BTC-ARIMA: 50.05
S. Colianni, S. Rosales and M. Signorotti [29]	-	-	-	-	BTC-BYS: 55.0 BTC-SVM: 53.5 BTC-LR: 86.0
X. Du, Z. Tang, J. Wu, K. Chen, Y. Cai [40]	-	-	(1 Day Ahead) BTC-ARIMA: 3.5206 BTC-BP: 3.504 ETH-ARIMA: 4.7814 ETH-BP: 4.7438	-	-
T. Muniye, S. Satapathy, M. Rout [41]	-	(1 Day Ahead) BTC-LSTM: 0.092 BTC-GRU: 0.075 (3 Days Ahead) BTC-LSTM: 0.079 BTC-GRU: 0.065	-	(1 Day Ahead) BTC-LSTM: 0.068 BTC-GRU: 0.065 (3 Days Ahead) BTC-LSTM: 0.057 BTC-GRU: 0.046	-

(*continued*)

Table 3. (*continued*)

Reference	MSE	RMSE	MAE	MAPE(%)	Accuracy(%)
M. Mudassir, S. Bennbaia, D. Unal, M. Hammoudeh [42]	-	**(End of Day)** BTC-ANN: 6.13 BTC-SVM: 2.37 BTC-SANN: 1.58 BTC-LSTM: 3.01	-	**(End of Day)** BTC-SVM: 1.44 **(7 Days Ahead)** BTC SANN: 2.88	BTC-SVM: 55.0 BTC-LSTM: 54.0 BTC-ANN: 57.0
Z. Chen, C. Li and W. Sun [45]	-	-	-	-	**(1 Day Ahead)** BTC-LR LDA: 65.3 BTC-RF: 51.0 BTC-LSTM: 57.0 **(5 Min Ahead)** BTC- LR LDA: 53.0 BTC-RF: 64.8 BTC-LSTM: 67.2
H. Jiang [43]	-	BTC-LR: 11175.563 BTC-KNN: 5774.448	-	-	-
P. Jay, V. Kalariya, P. Parmar, S. Tanwar, N. Kumar, M. Alazab [44]	BTC-MLP: 185950.356 ETH-MLP: 64.203 LTC-MLP: 12.210	BTC-MLP: 0.04438 ETH-MLP: 0.3900 LTC-MLP: .04097 BTC-LSTM: 0.4406 ETH-LSTM: 0.4849 LTC-LSTM:0.04068	BTC-MLP: 0.03062 ETH-MLP: 0.02710 LTC-MLP: .02677 BTC-LSTM: 0.03202 ETH-LSTM: 0.03481 LTC-LSTM: 0.02768	BTC-MLP: 3.06223 ETH-MLP: 2.70989 LTC-MLP: 2.67675 BTC-LSTM: 3.20205 ETH-LSTM: 3.48131 LTC-LSTM: 2.76838	-

4 Conclusion

Machine learning and Blockchain technology have attracted the attention of academics and practitioners and their real world applications are becoming increasingly visible to everyone. To understand the trend of machine learning techniques used in the prediction of cryptocurrency prices, in this research, we have identified and reviewed 24 research papers between 2014 and 2022. We hope this research provides practitioners and researchers with insight and future direction on these emerging technologies.

The results of the review presented in this paper have several significant implications. In the eight year time period of this review, more than half of the total research was done in the 2 years. There is a clear distinction between the performance of neural network-based models and classical statistical models in predicting the price and price movement direction prediction. While neural network-based models perform better when predicting the price movement direction, models like linear regression perform better when employed to predict the actual price.

Our classification and review model will provide other researchers with guidelines for future research. Applying other machine learning techniques that have not been investigated by other researchers while comparing their performance with models that have been used in the past can be an excellent topic for future research.

Acknowledgement. This work was supported by grant #2050883 from the National Science Foundation.

References

1. Nakamoto, S.: Bitcoin: a peer-to-peer electronic cash system (2008)
2. Coin Market Cap. https://coinmarketcap.com/currencies/bitcoin/. Accessed 23 Aug 2022
3. Bayer, D., Haber, S., Stornetta, W.S.: Improving the efficiency and reliability of digital time-stamping. Springer, New York, NY (1993). https://doi.org/10.1007/978-1-4613-9323-8_24
4. Haber, S., Stornetta, W.S.: How to time-stamp a digital document. J. Cryptol. **3**(2), 99–111 (1991)
5. BigchainDB. bigchaindb.com. Accessed 23 Aug 2022
6. Namecoin. namecoin.org/. Accessed 23 Aug 2022
7. Steemit. steemit.com. Accessed 23 Aug 2022
8. Jordan, M.I., Mitchell, T.M.: Machine learning: trends, perspectives, and prospects. Science **349**(6245), 255–260 (2017)
9. Machine Learning - Facebook Research, Facebook. https://research.facebook.com/research-areas/machine-learning/. Accessed 2022 Aug 2023
10. Kimoto, T., Asakawa, K., Yoda, M., Takeoka, M.: Stock market prediction system with modular neural networks. In: IJCNN International Joint Conference on Neural Networks, San Diego (1990)
11. Zhai, J., Cao, Y., Ding, X.: Data analytic approach for manipulation detection in stock market. Rev. Quant. Financ. Acc. **50**(3), 897–932 (2018)
12. Holub, M., Johnson, J.: Bitcoin research across disciplines. Inf. Soc. **34**(2), 114–126 (2018)
13. Shah, D., Zhang, K.: Bayesian regression and Bitcoin, In: 52nd Annual Allerton Conference on Communication, Control, and Computing, Monticello (2014)
14. Greaves, A., Au, B.: Using the bitcoin transaction graph to predict the price of bitcoin (2015)
15. Jang, H., Lee, J.: An empirical study on modeling and prediction of bitcoin prices with Bayesian neural networks based on blockchain information. IEEE **6**, 5427–5437 (2017)
16. Indera, N., Yassin, I., Zabidi, A., Rizman, Z.: Non-linear autoregressive with exogenous input (NARX) bitcoin price prediction model using PSO-optimized parameters and moving average technical indicators. J. Fundamental Appl. Sci. **9**(3S), 791 (2018)
17. Kim, Y.B., Kim, J.G., Kim, W., Im, J.H., Kim, T.: Predicting fluctuations in cryptocurrency transactions based on user comments and replies. PLoS ONE **11**(8), e0161197 (2016)
18. Nakano, M., Takahashi, A., Takahashi, S.: Bitcoin technical trading with artificial neural network. Physica A **510**, 587–609 (2018)

19. Alessandretti, L., ElBahrawy, A., Aiello, L.M., Baronchelli, A.: Machine Learning the Cryptocurrency Market. SSRN (2018)
20. Altan, A., Karasu, S., Bekiros, S.: Digital currency forecasting with chaotic meta-heuristic bio-inspired signal processing techniques. Chaos, Solitons Fractals **126**, 325–336 (2019)
21. Mallqui, D.C., Fernandes, R.A.: Predicting the direction, maximum, minimum and closing prices of daily Bitcoin exchange rate using machine learning techniques. Appl. Soft Comput. **75**, 596–606 (2019)
22. Li, T.R., Chamrajnagar, A.S., Fong, X.R., Rizik, N.R., Fu, F.: sentiment-based prediction of alternative cryptocurrency price fluctuations using gradient boosting tree model. Front. Phys. **7**, 98 (2019)
23. Ly, B., Timaul, D., Lukanan, A., Lau, J., Steinmetz, E.: Applying deep learning to better predict cryptocurrency trends. In: Midwest Instruction and Computing Symposium, Duluth (2018)
24. Velankar, S., Valecha, S., Maji, S.: Bitcoin price prediction using machine learning. In: 20th International Conference on Advanced Communication Technology, Chuncheon-si Gangwon-do (2018)
25. Jiang, Z., Liang, J.: Cryptocurrency portfolio management with deep reinforcement learning. In: Intelligent Systems Conference (IntelliSys), London (2017)
26. McNally, S., Roche, J., Caton, S.: Predicting the price of bitcoin using machine learning. In: 26th Euromicro International Conference on Parallel, Distributed and Network-based Processing (PDP), Cambridge (2018)
27. Kim, H.-M., Bock, G.-W., Lee, G.: Predicting ethereum prices using machine learning and block chain information. In: Americas' Conference on Information Systems (AMCIS) (2019)
28. Guo, T., Antulov-Fantulin, N.: Predicting short-term Bitcoin price fluctuations from buy and sell orders (2018)
29. Colianni, S., Rosales, S., Signorotti, M.: Algorithmic trading of cryptocurrency based on twitter sentiment analysis (2015)
30. Lamon, C., Nielsen, E., Redondo, E.: Cryptocurrency price prediction using news and social media sentiment (2017)
31. Koehrsen, W.: Introduction to Bayesian linear regression. https://towardsdatascience.com/int roduction-to-bayesian-linear-regression-e66e60791ea7. Accessed 16 Jul 2018
32. LeCun, Y., Haffner, P., Bottou, L., Bengio, Y.: Object recognition with gradient-based learning. In: Shape, contour and grouping in computer vision. LNCS, vol. 1681, pp. 319–345. Springer, Heidelberg (1999). https://doi.org/10.1007/3-540-46805-6_19
33. Hochreiter, S., Schmidhuber, J.: Long short-term memory. Neural Comput. **9**(8), 1735–1780 (1997)
34. Caruana, R., Karampatziakis, N., Yessenalina, A.: An empirical evaluation of supervised learning in high dimensions. In: ICML (2008)
35. Yin, H.S., Vatrapu, R.: A first estimation of the proportion of cybercriminal entities in the bitcoin ecosystem using supervised machine learning. In: 2017 IEEE International Conference on Big Data, Boston (2017)
36. Chen, W., Zheng, Z., Cui, J., Ngai, E., Zheng, P., Zhou, Y.: Detecting Ponzi schemes on ethereum: towards healthier blockchain technology. In: World Wide Web Conference, Lyon (2018)
37. Pichl, L., Kaizoji, T.: Volatility analysis of bitcoin price time series. Quant. Financ. Econ. **1**(4), 474–485 (2017)
38. Kurtulmus, A.B., Daniel, K.: Trustless machine learning contracts; evaluating and exchanging machine learning models on the ethereum blockchain (2018)
39. Kuo, T.-T., Ohno-Machado, L.: ModelChain: decentralized privacy-preserving healthcare predictive modeling framework on private blockchain networks (2018)

40. Du, X., et al.: A new hybrid cryptocurrency returns forecasting method based on multi-scale decomposition and an optimized extreme learning machine using the sparrow search algorithm. IEEE Access **10**, 60397–60411 (2022)
41. Awoke, T., et al.: Bitcoin price prediction and analysis using deep learning models. Commun. Softw. Netw. (2020)
42. Mudassir, M., et al.: Time series forecasting of Bitcoin prices using high dimensional features: a machine learning approach. Neural Comput. Appl., 1–15 (2020)
43. Jiang, H.: Cryptocurrency price forecasting based on shorttern trend KNN model. In: 2021 IEEE 3rd International Conference on Civil Aviation Safey and Information Technology (2021)
44. Jay, P., et al.: Stochastic neural networks for cryptocurrency price prediction. IEEE Access **8**, 82804–82818 (2020)
45. Chen, Z., Li, C., Sun, W.: Bitcoin Price prediction using machine learning: An approach to sample dimension engineering. J. Comput. Appl. Math. **365**, 112–395 (2020)
46. Oyedele et al.: Performance evaluation of deep learning and boosted trees for cryptocurrency closing price prediction. Expert Syst. Appl. **213** Part C 5 (2023)
47. Shaikh, I.A.K., Krishna, P.V., Biswal, S.G., Kumar, A.S., Baranidharan, S., Singh, K.: Bayesian optimization with stacked sparse autoencoder based cryptocurrency price prediction model. In: 2023 5th International Conference on Smart Systems and Inventive Technology (ICSSIT), Tirunelveli, India, pp. 653–658 (2023). https://doi.org/10.1109/ICSSIT55814.2023.10061153

A Secure Contact Tracing Method Using Smart Contracts with Considering Privacy

Kazumasa Omote[1,2]([✉]) and Tatsuhiro Fukuda[1]

[1] University of Tsukuba, Tennodai 1-1-1, Tsukuba 305-8573, Japan
`omote@risk.tsukuba.ac.jp`
[2] National Institute of Information and Communications Technology,
4-2-1 Nukui-Kitamachi, Koganei, Tokyo 184-8795, Japan

Abstract. Contact tracing, which uses smartphones to track the behavioral history of device owners, is used for infection control and crime control. On the other hand, contact tracing collects personal information, such as location data, which raises privacy issues. Actually, in the case of centralized systems, what data is collected is a black box. Against this background, there are many studies on contact tracing combined with a decentralized manageable blockchain. However, many studies need to consider the forgery of data before it is stored in the blockchain (i.e., blockchain oracle problem). Lv et al. consider such data forgery, but their approach requires users to manage many private keys. In this study, we propose a contact tracing method that prevents the forgery of data before it is stored in the blockchain and protects user privacy by encrypting location data. We implement our method using a smart contract and a smartphone to demonstrate the feasibility of the proposed method. The proposed method has lower key management costs than the existing method of Lv et al.

1 Introduction

Contact tracing is a technology that uses smartphone applications to track people who come into contact with the device owner and the locations visited by the owner, and is mainly used in the control of infectious diseases such as COVID-19. Contact tracing can also be used to track people's movements, which can be used to assist police investigations and reinforce eyewitness testimony in crime control. For example, Singapore is attempting to use applications for contact tracing in criminal investigations [2]. On the other hand, contact tracing collects personal information, such as location data, which raises privacy issues. In particular, in the case of a centralized system, there are concerns about what kind of data is collected and whether the collected data is used appropriately.

Contact tracing research is conducted using a decentralized manageable blockchain that satisfies tamper resistance and data transparency while meeting with privacy protection. However, most studies focus only on user privacy and

Q. Wang et al. (Eds.): ICBC 2023, LNCS 14206, pp. 89–103, 2023.
https://doi.org/10.1007/978-3-031-44920-8_6

do not consider the forgery of data before it is stored in the blockchain (i.e., blockchain oracle problem). Also, only some studies deal with tracking the contact person and the visited location. Lv et al. [9] consider the forgery of data before it is stored in the blockchain and deal with tracking contact persons and visited locations. In this method, a user broadcasts a public key to surrounding users as a challenge and receives location data as a response, thereby surrounding users to assure the validity of the initiating user's information. However, this approach requires a different public key for each data record, so the user must maintain many secret keys.

In this study, we propose a contact tracing method that prevents the forgery of data before it is stored in the blockchain and protects the user's privacy. We implement our method using a smart contract and a smartphone to demonstrate the feasibility. By combining challenge-response and smart contract verification, the proposed method makes it possible to detect the forgery of data before it is stored in the blockchain and protects privacy by encrypting location data. In addition, the proposed method uses blockchain to manage encryption keys, which reduces the key management cost compared to existing methods.

2 Preliminary

2.1 Blockchain

Blockchain constitutes a P2P network where all peers are equal, and there is no single point of failure [11]. Transaction data generated on the network is compiled into blocks, which are connected to form a single blockchain. Once data is recorded in a blockchain, it is difficult to tamper with that data.

Blockchains can be divided into several types depending on whether or not there is an administrator or access control. Public-type blockchains do not have an administrator, and anyone can join the network. Private blockchains have a single administrator; only authorized nodes can join the network. The consortium type has multiple administrators; only authorized nodes can join the network. Public blockchains require fees for sending transactions and executing smart contracts, while private and consortium blockchains do not. In general, consortium and private types are permission-based blockchains. Recently, however, permissionless consortium blockchains have attracted attention [12]. The proposed scheme is designed to use such a permissionless consortium blockchain.

2.2 Smart Contract

A smart contract is a program that runs on the blockchain and automatically executes a specific contract without an intermediary. The execution of smart contracts is recorded, thus ensuring transparency of the contracts and their outputs. In addition, since smart contracts are recorded on the block, once deployed on the blockchain, the contract cannot be deleted or changed. Ethereum, a public-type chain, and Hyperledger Fabric, a consortium-type blockchain, are well-known blockchains that employ smart contracts.

2.3   Contact Tracing

Contact tracing is a technology that uses applications on devices such as smart-phones to record who contacts the device owner and where the device owner has visited to record the device owner's behavior and to track users who contact the device owner. It is mainly used in the control of infectious diseases such as COVID-19. It is also used in Singapore for criminal investigations. Contact tracing can be divided into two main types; one focuses on the individual, which traces the person who contacts the device owner, and the other focuses on the location, which traces the places visited by the device owner.

Tahir et al. [14] analyzed various COVID-19 contact tracing applications used in 32 countries worldwide. In Japan, the COVID-19 Contact-Confirming Application (COCOA) was developed by the Japanese Ministry of Health, Labor and Welfare [10]. The ID is generated based on a random code called a date/time key that is generated once a day and updated after a certain period. When a user becomes a positive patient, the user registers the date/time key and other information to the notification server through the application. Using the application, other users can check whether they are in close contact with positive patients.

3   Related Work

Many studies on blockchain-based contact tracing have focused on tamper-resistance and user address anonymity in the blockchain. Garg et al. [4] proposed an IoT-based anonymous contact tracing method using the anonymity of blockchain, which was implemented and evaluated using Ethereum and smart-phones. In this method, contact tracing of moving objects is achieved by attaching contactless readable RFID tags to moving objects such as pets and cars and installing RFID readers at building entrances and highway toll stations. Blockchain is used as storage. Klaine et al. [7] proposed a contact tracing method that ensures user privacy by allowing users to generate IDs using timestamps periodically. Users broadcast their IDs and maintain a list of received IDs. If a person becomes a positive patient, medical institutions publish all the IDs of the patient to the blockchain so that users can confirm whether or not they are in close contact persons with a positive patient. Aslam et al. [1] proposed a contact tracing method that combines a consortium blockchain and fuzzy inference to infer a user's COVID-19 infection status. Medical institutions encrypt and record the user's infection status on the blockchain, and a trusted government agency records at-risk areas where positive patients are found. Liu et al. [8] propose a privacy-preserving tracing solution for contact tracing systems using crypto-graphic techniques (i.e., non-interactive zero-knowledge proofs and aggregated multi-signatures). However, these studies do not record location data, which is necessary to identify the infection route and location.

Xu et al. [15] proposed a contact tracing method that protects the privacy of user IDs. In this method, a blockchain address is generated each time that partially contains the location data, and the location data, encrypted with the

CA's public key, is recorded in the blockchain. When a user becomes a positive patient, a trusted tracing agency receives the private key from the CA, decrypts the recorded data, and searches for concentrated contact persons based on the decrypted data. Zhang et al. [16] proposed a contact tracing method that combines two types of blockchains, a public blockchain and a private blockchain, to protect user privacy. Users record their information and location to the private blockchain through fog nodes installed in various locations. However, these studies record location data but only indirectly record the contact person, making it costly to identify the contact person.

Lv et al. [9] consider the forgery of data before it is stored in the blockchain and propose, implement, and evaluate a privacy-preserving contact tracing method for publishing user location data on a blockchain. A user broadcasts a public key as a challenge to surrounding users and receives as a response a contact history of a specific location and a signature on the contact history of the responding users. This means that other users can guarantee the legitimacy of the information recorded by the initiating user and prevent data forgery by the user. In addition, the user generates multiple private/public key pairs and uses a randomly selected public key as a challenge each time, thereby reducing the link between the ID information and the user. However, managing many private/public key pairs is necessary to protect user privacy locally.

In other researches, Bari et al. [3] proposed a data storage system for contact tracing using blockchain with role-based access control; Hasan et al. [6] bridged the gap between on- and off-chain data by introducing on-chain registered oracle and integrated it into the Ethereum blockchain; Rashid et al. [13] built a contact tracing system that combines Hyperledger Fabric and the InterPlanetary File System (IPFS). However, these studies do not mention a concrete contact tracing method.

4   Our Method

4.1   Overview

We propose a contact tracing method that prevents the forgery of data before it is stored in the blockchain and protects user privacy by encrypting location data. Similar to the method of Lv et al., a user i receives location data and blockchain address from surrounding users using challenge-response authentication. By recording such contact history, surrounding users guarantee the location of user i. The location data is encrypted using a symmetric key encryption scheme, and the encryption key is a random key generated by the user. The random key is updated periodically. Using a blockchain for key management, the keys managed locally by the user are minimized to only a private/public key pair and a single random key. For users surrounding user i, we assume that the number of correctly behaving users is more significant than the that of malicious users. Figure 1 shows an overview of the proposed method.

The proposed method consists of four steps: (1) user registration, (2) recording contact history between users based on challenge-response authentication,

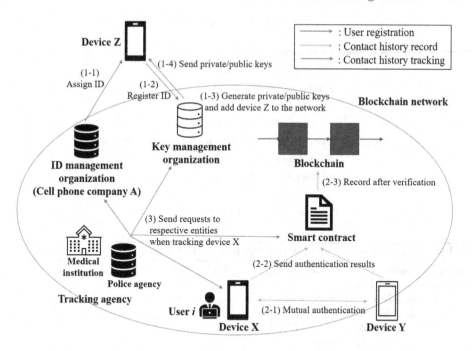

Fig. 1. Overview of the proposed method

(3) updating random keys, and (4) tracking the activity history performed by a tracking agency based on the information recorded in the blockchain. We describe each step in detail in this section. The notation used in this paper is shown in Table 1.

4.2   Entity

User has a smartphone or wearable device and uses an application installed on the device to communicate via Bluetooth with surrounding users. The user has the role of both a challenger, who sends a challenge, and a responder, who returns a response to the challenge. To record the contact history obtained through Bluetooth communication in the blockchain, the user receives an ID from an identity management organization and then receives a private/public key from a key management organization by sending the ID to the key management organization. In addition, the user generates a random key to encrypt the location data. The user then keeps these keys.

ID management organization is a trusted authority that issues IDs to users to participate in the blockchain network and manages the IDs by linking ID to the user's personal information. The actual organization is assumed to be a cell phone company, which grants the user an ID and a phone number when they sign up for a smartphone.

Table 1. Notation

Notation	Definition
$addr_i$	Blockchain address of user i
pk_i	Public key of user i
sk_i	Private key of user i
vk_{it}	Random key at time t for user i
$Enc_{key}()$	Encryption function using encryption key key
$H()$	Hash function
c	Challenge (random number)
t	Timestamp
L_t	Location data at time t

Algorithm 1. Record contact history: reportContactLog

Require: $addr_j$, j's signature, $Enc_{vk_{it}}(L_t)$, $H(L_t)$, t, c
Ensure: True / False
  if Sender address $!= addr_j$ **and** $addr_j$ is registered in the network **then**
    Obtain address from the signature
    if Retrieved address $== addr_j$ **then**
      Record contact history
    end if
  end if

Key management organization is a trusted authority that, after receiving the ID from the user, is responsible for generating the user's private/public key, passing it to the user, and registering the user in the blockchain network. It manages the user's ID and public key by linking them together.

Tracking agency is intended for police agencies and medical institutes to track the activity history of specific users based on the information recorded in the blockchain. This agency works with identity and key management organizations to identify users and track their location.

4.3   Smart Contract Functions

The information recorded in the blockchain shall be available to everyone, and only blockchain participants shall have access to the smart contracts. The contact history in the proposed method includes the blockchain address of the transaction sender, the blockchain address of the user contacted by the sender, encrypted location information, the hash value of location data, and the timestamp. The smart contract functions are as follows.

Record Contact History: ReportContactLog. This function records the contact history between users. The function verifies that the sender (user i) has

---

Algorithm 2. Store random key: storeKey

Require: $Enc_{pk_i}(vk_{it})$, t
Ensure: True / False
   Record timestamp and encrypted random key

---

contacted another user (user j) participating in the blockchain and verifies the signature of user j to ensure that the contact history is not forged by the sender i. Specifically, after obtaining the blockchain address $addr_j$ from the signature[1] in the contact history, this smart contract checks that the address matches $addr_j$ in the contact history. If the verification result is valid, it records the contact history.

Store Random Key: StoreKey. This function allows the user to store the random key. By storing it in the blockchain in this way, the user can decrypt the past random key at any time using his/her private key.

4.4   User Registration

Users take the following steps to join the blockchain network. The user's personal information is not directly linked to the address but is managed through an ID, which prevents the user from being identified without the consent of multiple organizations and ensures the user's anonymity.

1. User i registers personal information with an ID management organization and receives an ID issued by such an organization and its signature. The ID management organization is assumed to be a cell phone company.
2. User i sends the ID and its signature to the key management organization.
3. After verifying that the signature is generated by the ID management organization, the key management organization generates the private/public key and adds user i to the blockchain network.
4. The key management organization sends the generated private/public key to user i.

4.5   Recording of Contact History

The user records the contact history by following the steps below. Note that these processes are performed automatically by a smartphone in the background; the user only needs to start the application. The flow of recording contact history is shown in Fig. 2, where user i is the challenger and user j is the responder.

1. Using Bluetooth, user i broadcasts a random number c as a challenge to the surrounding area.

---

[1] Strictly speaking, the public key is recovered from the ECDSA signature, and the blockchain address is obtained by computing the address from the public key.

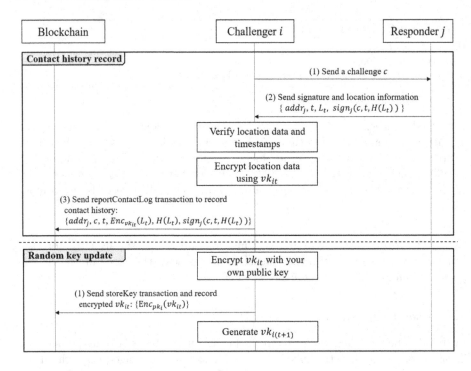

Fig. 2. Flow of recording contact history and updating random keys

2. Upon receiving the challenge, user j returns his address $addr_j$, timestamp t, location data L_t, and their signature to user i as a response.
3. User i verifies whether the location data is within Bluetooth range and the timestamp is the current time.
4. After the verification result is valid, user i encrypts the location data with his/her own random key vk_{it}.
5. User i sends $addr_j$, c, t the encrypted L_t, the hash of L_t, and user j's signature through a transaction.
6. The smart contract verifies the signature. The contact history is recorded in the blockchain if the verification result is valid.

4.6   Updating of Random Key

The user updates the random key vk_{it} periodically, e.g., once daily. The old random key is encrypted with his/her public key and recorded in the blockchain. The flow of random key updates is shown at the bottom of Fig. 2. The encrypted random key is used when providing location data to the tracking agency. Specifically, the user decrypts the corresponding random key with his/her private key and provides it to the tracking agency. By updating the random key periodically, the location data obtained by the tracking agency is kept to a minimum, and the user's privacy is protected.

4.7   Tracking of Behavior History

Tracking agencies, including police and medical institutions, track the behavioral history of a particular address in order to enhance eyewitness testimony and identify the route of infection. After obtaining the contact history corresponding to an address from the blockchain, two steps are performed: (1) individual identification and (2) decryption of the location data. Since the address of a close contact person is included in the contact history, such an address can be identified from the contact history.

(1) Individual Identification

1. The tracking agency queries the key management organization for the ID corresponding to the tracked address and obtains it together with the signature of the key management organization.
2. Based on the obtained ID and its signature, the tracking agency contacts the ID management organization to obtain the user information corresponding to the ID and contacts the user.

(2) Decryption of the Location Data. After identifying the user corresponding to the Blockchain address, the following steps are performed.

1. Based on the address and timestamp, the tracking agency obtains a list of encrypted random keys from the blockchain to decrypt the location data.
2. The tracking agency sends a list of encrypted random keys to the user.
3. The user decrypts the random key using his/her private key and sends the random key to the tracking agency.
4. The tracking agency verifies that the random key provided is correct. Specifically, it re-encrypts the random key using the user's public key and metadata and compares it to the encrypted data recorded in the blockchain.
5. The tracking agency decrypts the location data using a random key and verifies that the location data is not forged. Specifically, the tracking agency compares the hash value of the decrypted location data with the hash value of the location data recorded in the blockchain.

5   Demonstration Experiment

To demonstrate the feasibility of the proposed method, we implement the application and measure the time required for communication using two actual iPhone devices.

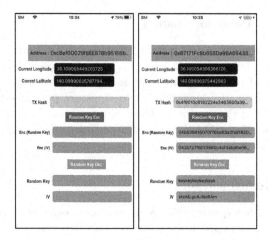

Fig. 3. Screenshot of the created application (left: Peripheral side, right: Central side)

5.1   Environment

We used Rinkeby testnet[2], one of Ethereum's test networks, and Metamask, an Ethereum wallet browser extension, to implement smart contracts utilizing the solidity language. The iPhone 6 and 8 are used as communication devices, and Swift and Xcode are used to create the application.

The user encrypts the random key with their public key and records it in the blockchain. Each user has two private/public key pairs[3], one for signing and one for encrypting. The specific elliptic curve is secp256r1; more precisely, the ECIES (Elliptic Curve Integrated Encryption Scheme) is used for encryption, and ECDSA (Elliptic Curve Digital Signature Algorithm) is used for the signature. The random key is used for AES-CBC (key length 128 bits), symmetric key encryption. Note that since the CBC mode requires an initial vector separately from the encryption key, the encryption key and the initialization vector are encrypted.

5.2   Experimental Flow

1. We install the created application on two iPhones and confirm that the contact history is recorded in the blockchain after the two iPhones communicate.
2. After the encrypted random key is recorded in the blockchain, we verify that the random key can be decrypted with the private key and that the location data can be decrypted by that random key.

---

[2] Certainly, the same demonstration experiment can be conducted on the latest Goerli Testnet.

[3] To realize two key pairs of private/public key for signing and encrypting with a single key pair, please refer to [5].

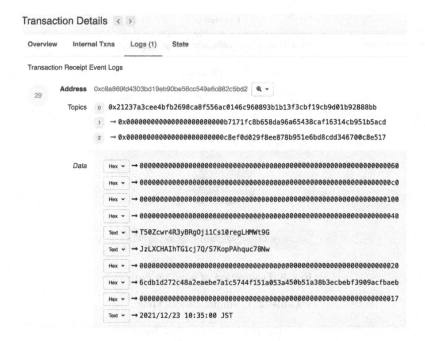

Fig. 4. Contents of reportContactLog

3. We measure the average time for ten Bluetooth connections to communicate, from sending the challenge to receiving the response.

In this implementation, the "Central" device, which plays the role of server in Bluetooth communication, and the "Peripheral" device, which plays the role of client, are separated for each device. We use two types of iPhones as the central device, So the measurements are taken with the iPhone 6 and 8 as the Central devices.

5.3   Execution Results

The screens of our application are shown in Fig. 3. The left side of the figure shows the screen of the Peripheral side that returns a response, and the right side of the figure shows the screen of the Central side that sends a challenge, receives a response, and then sends a transaction to record the contact history. The Central screen records the contact history, the ciphertext of the random key and initial vector, and their decrypted values.

Record of Contact History. Figure 4 is a screenshot of Etherescan, showing the contents of a transaction containing the contact history generated between devices. Specifically, the first line of Topics shows the sender's address, and the second line shows the user's address who returned the response. The fifth and

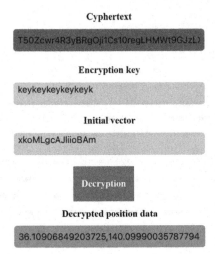

Fig. 5. Decryption of location data

Table 2. Communication Time

Central side	Average time (sec)
iPhone 6	8.85
iPhone 8	7.51

sixth lines of Data are the encrypted location data, the eighth line is the hash value of the location data, and the tenth line is the timestamp. Anyone can confirm that the contact history is recorded on the blockchain from these values.

Decryption of Location Data. The encrypted random key can be easily viewed by anyone through Etherscan. The value of the random key obtained by decrypting the value recorded there is shown at the bottom of the screen on the Central side in Fig. 3. Then, the result of decrypting the location data in Fig. 4 is shown in Fig. 5. You can see that the location data is appropriately decrypted.

Communication Time. The results of communication time are shown in Table 2. The results show that the average time from Bluetooth connection to receiving a response after sending a challenge was about 8 s. For example, given that the definition of a close contact person in Japan is a contact of 15 min or longer, the proposed method can be used without any problem.

6   Discussion

6.1   Data Forgery by Users

When user i and j communicate, we consider the forgery of data before it is stored in the blockchain. In this case, there are two possible patterns: forgery by user i, the sender of the challenge, and forgery by user j, the user who returns the response.

Consider the case where user i performs forgery. Since the smart contract performs verification based on user j's signature, user i cannot forge the times-tamp and address, but user i can falsify the location data since user i encrypts it. However, the hash value of the location data provided by user j is recorded in the blockchain. Therefore, forgery by user i can be detected by comparing the hash values when the location data is decrypted.

Consider the case where user j performs forgery. Forgery by user j can be detected by user i, who receives the response by performing verification based on his location data and current time. In that case, no transaction is sent, so data forgery cannot be performed.

Note, however, that if multiple users collude, e.g., user i and j collude to record false location data, the data can be forged by the users.

6.2   Notification of Close Contact Persons

If our method is used in infectious disease control, it is necessary to notify close contact persons who had contact with the positive patient. There are two possible notification patterns for close contact persons.

- The medical institution publishes the addresses of close contact persons or positive patients on the blockchain. Each user checks if they are a close contact person.
- The medical institution contacts the close contact person using the method described in Sect. 4.7.1 based on the address of the close contact person.

Considering user privacy, it is better to use the former, except in an emergency.

6.3   Update Private/Public Key

In the proposed method, there are cases where the anonymity of the user address is lost after the user is tracked. A possible solution to this problem is for the user to request the key management authority to update their private/public key. Specifically, the user obtains a signature for their public key from the tracking agency, sends the signature and their signature for the tracking agency's public key to the key management organization, and receives a new private/public key from the key management organization. The tracking agency's signature prevents the user from updating the public key carelessly, and the user's signature prevents the tracking agency from updating the key on its own. In this way, the anonymity of the user address is maintained even once tracking has taken place.

6.4 Use Case

The proposed method could be used in the medical field as a countermeasure against infectious diseases, as in the case of the COCOA application, such as notification of close contact persons and identification of infection routes. We also consider its use in crime control. In the proposed method, location data is encrypted and recorded in the blockchain, so the user cannot be identified from the location data. Therefore, the following utilization of the system can efficiently conduct criminal investigations.

- It is possible to identify people who were at the scene of the incident. For example, when user j is identified, the person at the crime scene can be identified in the chain based on j's contact history.
- It can be used as evidence. If you are suspected of being in a place where you can authenticate with surrounding users, you can prove where you were.

7 Conclusion

In this study, we propose a contact tracing method that prevents the forgery of data before it is stored in the blockchain and protects user privacy by encrypting location data. By combining challenge-response and verification with smart contracts, we make it possible to detect the forgery of data before it is stored in the blockchain. In addition, the encryption keys used to encrypt location data are managed by a blockchain, which reduces key management costs compared to existing research. Furthermore, we demonstrated the feasibility of the proposed method by implementing it using a smartphone and Ethereum smart contract.

Since the proposed method needs to be used by many users, it is necessary to incentivize users to cooperate. It is also required to address the issue of scalability of transactions, which increases as the number of users increases. We plan to study these issues in the future.

Acknowledgement. This work was supported by Grant-in-Aid for Challenging Exploratory Research (22K19768).

References

1. Aslam, B., Javed, A.R., Chakraborty, C., Nebhen, J., Raqib, S., Rizwan, M.: Blockchain and ANFIS Empowered IoMT Application for Privacy Preserved Contact Tracing in COVID-19 Pandemic. Personal and Ubiquitous Computing, pp. 1–17 (2021)
2. BBC News: Singapore Reveals Covid Privacy Data Available to Police. https://www.bbc.com/news/world-asia-55541001. January 5, 2021
3. Bari, N., Qamar, U., Khalid, A.: Efficient Contact Tracing for Pandemics using Blockchain. Informatics in Medicine Unlocked, vol. 26 (2021)
4. Garg, L., Chukwu, E., Nasser, N., Chakraborty, C., Garg, G.: Anonymity preserving IoT-based COVID-19 and other infectious disease contact tracing model. IEEE Access, vol. 8, August 2020

5. Hanaoka, G., Sakai, Y., Shimizu, T., Shimoyama, T., Shin, S.H.: A setup-free threshold encryption scheme for the bitcoin protocol and its applications. IEICE Trans. Fundamentals Electron. Commun. Comput. Sci. **E103.A**(1), 150–164 (2020)
6. Hasan, H.R., Salah, K., Jayaraman, R., Yaqoob, I., Omar, M., Ellahham, S.: COVID-19 contact tracing using blockchain. IEEE Access **9**, 62956–62971 (2021)
7. Klaine, P.V., Zhang, L., Zhou, B., Sun, Y., Xu, H., Imran, M.: Privacy-preserving contact tracing and public risk assessment using blockchain for COVID-19 pandemic. IEEE Internet Things Mag. **3**(3), 58–63 (2020)
8. Liu, M., Zhang, Z., Chai, W., Wang, B.: Privacy-preserving COVID-19 contact tracing solution based on blockchain. Comput. Stand. Interf. **83** (2023)
9. Lv, W., Wu, S., Jiang, C., Cui, Y., Qiu, X., Zhang, Y.: Towards large-scale and privacy-preserving contact tracing in COVID-19 pandemic: a blockchain perspective. IEEE Trans. Network Sci. Eng. **9**(1), 282–298 (2022)
10. Ministry of Health, Labour and Welfare, "COVID-19 Contact-Confirming Application (COCOA)". https://www.mhlw.go.jp/stf/seisakunitsuite/bunya/cocoa_00007.html
11. Nakamoto, S.: Bitcoin: a peer-to-peer electronic cash system (2009)
12. Omote, K.: Does private blockchain make sense? In: The 41st IEEE International Conference on Consumer Electronics (ICCE), IEEE, pp. 1–3 (2023)
13. Rashid, M.M., Choi, P., Lee, S.-H., Kwon, K.-R.: Block-HPCT: blockchain enabled digital health passports and contact tracing of infectious diseases like COVID-19. Sensors **22**(11), 4256 (2022)
14. Tahir, S., Tahir, H., Sajjad, A., Rajarajan, M., Khan, F.: Privacy-preserving COVID-19 contact tracing using blockchain. J. Commun. Networks **23**(5), 360–373 (2021)
15. Xu, H., Zhang, L., Onireti, O., Fang, Y., Buchananm, W.J., Imran, M.A.: Beep-Trace: blockchain-enabled privacy-preserving contact tracing for COVID-19 pandemic and beyond. IEEE Internet Things J. **8**(5), September 2020
16. Zhang, C., Xu, C., Sharif, K., Zhu, L.: Privacy-preserving contact tracing in 5G-integrated and blockchain-based medical applications. Comput. Stand. Interfaces **77**, August 2021

Comparison of Smart Contract Platforms from the Perspective of Developers

Ammar Voloder[✉] and Monika di Angelo

Technische Universität Wien, Vienna, Austria
ammarvoloder@gmail.com, monika.di.angelo@tuwien.ac.at

Abstract. Blockchain technologies promise to transform businesses by offering benefits like efficiency, transparency, fewer intermediaries, streamlined processes, and cost savings. With several public and private blockchain options available, companies and developers face the challenge of choosing a suitable platform for their needs. Ethereum has emerged as the most popular platform for the development of blockchain programs, but alternatives such as Algorand, Cardano, EOS, and Neo have also gained traction. We assess these five platforms from a developer's perspective. Based on a catalog of criteria and metrics, we compare the platforms regarding their key features, including practical aspects like availability of documentation and ease of installation. We specify three use cases that are characteristic of blockchain applications: fungible tokens, non-fungible tokens, and a basic supply chain. By implementing these use cases on all platforms and logging the effort as well as any incidents, we identify their strengths and weaknesses in a way that supports developers in choosing an appropriate platform.

Keywords: blockchain · criteria · evaluation · implementation · metric

1 Introduction

Smart contract platforms offer a range of benefits that can improve efficiency, transparency, security, and cost-effectiveness for companies. Their use promises to streamline processes and to reduce the need for intermediaries. By providing a permanent and transparent record of transactions, one can develop applications where the parties do not need to trust each other.

There are several public and private blockchains that companies and developers can choose from. While a public blockchain is the natural choice for applications of general interest, private blockchains may be preferable for a consortium of companies. However, even consortia tend to rely on public blockchains for automatically enforcing inter-company agreements.[1]

---

[1] https://www.ey.com/en_gl/innovation/how-public-blockchains-are-making-private-blockchains-obsolete.

Q. Wang et al. (Eds.): ICBC 2023, LNCS 14206, pp. 104–118, 2023.
https://doi.org/10.1007/978-3-031-44920-8_7

Ethereum is the most popular platform for smart contracts regarding the number of developers[2] and contracts[3], by far. However, interesting alternatives emerged in recent years that are worth considering when developing smart contracts.

Aims and Methods. The goal of this work is to guide developers in choosing an appropriate platform for their application. It addresses the research question: What are the main strengths and weaknesses of the selected platforms from the perspective of developers when implementing an application? To this end, we propose an approach that facilitates the systematic comparison of smart contract platforms.

Our main contributions are

- a catalog of criteria (based on [2,5]) that focuses on the development of smart contracts,
- the definition of metrics addressing the implementation effort,
- the specification of three characteristic use cases,
- the implementation of the use cases on the five platforms Algorand, Cardano, EOS, Ethereum, and Neo, logging the progress as well as obstacles,
- a structured comparative evaluation of these platforms based on the criteria and the implementation logs.

For the code of the three use cases for the five platforms, see https://github.com/ammarvoloder/5x3.

2   Criteria for Platform Comparison

To compare smart contract platforms, a collection of appropriate criteria is essential. Regarding conceptual aspects, we select features that a platform should provide in sufficient quality to enable the development of smart contracts. For practical aspects, we define exemplary use cases, implement them on all platforms, and apply metrics designed to compare the implementation effort.

2.1   Catalog of Conceptual Criteria

Bareis et al. [2] compare smart contract platforms based on criteria obtained by an extensive literature search. The catalog covers technological as well as developmental aspects and serves the purpose of a general comparison well. We restructure it and add further categories that are important for our focus on development.

To emphasize the development perspective, we consider the findings of Bosu et al. [5], who identify *the lack of supporting materials* as the main challenge reported by blockchain developers, in particular immature and unreliable tools,

---

[2] https://cointelegraph.com/news/ethereum-dominates-among-developers-but-competitors-growing-faster.

[3] https://www.alchemy.com/overviews/ethereum-statistics.

Table 1. Catalog of Conceptual Criteria for Platform Comparison

Group	Technical Perspective	Development Perspective
Project	Objectives Origin and Organization Governance	
Blockchain Properties	Consensus Protocol Interoperability	Chain Availability Permission Type **Local Blockhain Setup**
Documentation and Support		Language Support Documentation
Extended Documentation		Community **Exemplary Contracts** **Educational Material**
Platform Development		**Tools + Testing** Standards

documentation being not user-friendly, and learning materials and tutorials being rare. Moreover, automated testing is mentioned as a primary need. Similarly, Zou et al. [27] argue for the need of good security testing and best practice examples. Table 1 presents the redesigned catalog employed in our study, with our additions to [2] marked in bold.

2.2 Assessing the Implementation Effort

We use four indicators for comparing implementation efforts: lines of code, the time spent, the level of experience required, and the number of issues/obstacles encountered.

The length of a contract in **lines of code** does not necessarily reflect its complexity. However, more lines are harder to handle than fewer. An implementation that can be kept short by relying on platform-specific primitives and libraries is easier to maintain and offers less potential for security issues. In our study, the contract length also indicates how well a platform supports the use case.

The **time spent** on a task probably is not the most relevant criterion when selecting a suitable blockchain. But it may indicate how steep the learning curve is and how difficult it is to start using a platform. Time depends on subjective factors like the developer's experience, and thus is not an absolute measure. However, as all use cases have been implemented by the first author, it allows us to compare the chains from a developer's perspective in a relative manner.

The **experience level** required for a particular use case and chain has been assessed by the first author, who is about to finish a master's program in software engineering and who has worked as a software engineer and blockchain developer (token applications, supply chain management) in multi-national companies for several years. Low experience (0–3 years) refers to a developer familiar with the basics of software engineering who is able to tackle simple tasks. Medium experience (3–5 years) refers to a person with a solid knowledge of software engineering, who is familiar with various technologies and therefore can grasp the basics of a new technology quickly. Finally, high experience (more than 5 years) refers to a developer with a deep knowledge of software engineering practices, who can utilize multiple platforms, tools, and technologies to design, plan, and implement complex tasks.

Finally, we count the **number of difficulties and issues** encountered for each use case and chain. These comprise the lack of adequate chain-specific documentation, non-existing sample code, inactive community, compatibility issues regarding the OS, and any code-related limitations (like compiler issues).

To facilitate the qualitative comparison in Table 4, we trisect the range of each metric and label the parts by $+$, $\circ$, and $-$. The thresholds in Table 2 have been set to balance the three parts as well as to reflect our expectations of what is acceptable.

Table 2. Metrics for the Implementation Effort

category	$+$	$-$	$\circ$
lines of code (LOC)	< 100	> 300	otherwise
time [hours]	< 10	> 20	otherwise
experience required (XP)	low	high	medium
issues	≤ 5	> 10	otherwise

3 Use Cases

To assess the development effort, we define three uses cases: a fungible token, a non-fungible token (NFT), and a simple supply chain management.

3.1 Token

Fungible tokens are blockchain tokens that have either a fixed supply or follow a specific and transparent supply schedule. Furthermore, they are interchangeable and equal in value. Tokens are governed by a smart contract and may have functionalities beyond the exchange of value. The use case is based on [8,13].

Scenario:

1. A token "SimpleToken" with symbol "STK" and a fixed supply is created.
2. The creator is checked for holding 1000 STK.
3. A new address is created and verified to have a balance of 0 STK.
4. 300 STK tokens are transferred to the new address.
5. The new address is verified to hold 300 STK tokens.
6. The creator is verified to hold 700 STK tokens.

3.2 NFT

A non-fungible token (NFT) is a unique digital asset stored on the blockchain. Individual NFTs are not directly interchangeable, as they may represent assets of different type and value. In addition, the metadata of an NFT may contain information that determines its appearance, scarcity, utility, and other factors affecting its value. NFTs can also be used to record the ownership of real-world items. The use case is based on [8,9,13].

Scenario:

1. A single token "NFTToken" is minted.
2. A new address is created and verified to have 0 NFTtoken.
3. The NFTToken is transferred to the new address.
4. The new address is verified to be the owner now.
5. The creator of the token should not possess it anymore.

3.3 Supply Chain Management

Supply chain management controls the flow of goods and services between multiple organizations and locations. Typical parties are producers, suppliers, freight forwarders, warehouses, distributors, and retailers. Traceable and transparent supply chains are motivated by the need for the attestation of product origin, quality and identity, or to certify the compliance with international regulations, standards and certifications. The use case is based on [7,10,14,19,20].

Actors in a coffee supply chain:

1. *Farmers* harvest, process, pack, and sell coffee beans to distributors.
2. *Distributors* buy coffee beans from farmers and ship them to retailers.
3. *Retailers* receive coffee beans and make them available to consumers.
4. *Consumers* purchase coffee beans from retailers.

States of the supply chain: harvested, processed, packed, for sale, sold, shipped, received, purchased.

Scenario:

1. Farmers harvest coffee beans and mark them as *harvested*.
2. Farmers process harvested beans and mark them as *processed*.
3. Farmers pack processed beans and mark them as *packed*.
4. To sell coffee, farmers mark packed beans as *for sale*.
5. Distributors buy beans and set their state to *sold*.
6. Distributors ship sold coffee beans and set their state to *shipped*.
7. Retailors mark shipped beans as *received*.
8. Customers purchase received coffee beans, which changes their state to *purchased*.

4   Selection of Smart Contract Platforms

Websites like www.coingecko.com list a few hundred blockchains supporting smart contracts, with Ethereum being the most prominent one. To illustrate our approach, we select five of the economically more successful projects (as judged by their market cap) that are both public and designed for general purpose applications. To demonstrate our approach on diverse blockchains, we discard forks. We concentrate on blockchains backed by communities and companies that actually want developers to use it, in order to ensure sufficient support regarding tools and documentation. After a preliminary feasibility study, we finally settled for Algorand, Cardano, EOS, Ethereum, and Neo.

5   Implementation Effort

5.1   Development Stack

Table 3 specifies the software stacks required to implement the three use cases on each platform. For the actual code see https://github.com/ammarvoloder/5x3.

Table 3. Software Stacks Required to Operate the Platforms

Algorand	Node v16.13.2	npm 8.4.1	Sandbox no release	algod v3.4.2 stable	postgres v13.6	Docker Desktop 4.6.0
Cardano	WSL 2	Ubuntu 20.04 LTS	GHCup Haskell v.0.1.17.8	ghc v8.10.7	cabal v.3.6.2.0	
EOS	WSL 2	Ubuntu 20.04 LTS	EOSIO binaries v2.1.0-1	EOSIO cdt v1.8.0-1		
Ethereum	Node v16.13.2	npm v8.4.1	Truffle v5.4.32	Solidity v0.8.11	Ganache v2.5.4	
NEO	Node v16.13.2	npm v8.4.1	neo-express v.3.1.46	.NET 5.0 SDK		

5.2   Assessing the Effort

Evaluating the logs [24] recorded during the implementation phase with the metrics in Table 2, we obtain the results in Table 4. For Cardano, we did not succeed in completing the third use case (supply chain) within the allotted time of 30 h. Therefore, no LOC metric is given.

According to the total number of pluses and minuses, the use cases get more complex from left to right. All use cases taken together, Ethereum requires the least effort, with eight pluses and four mediums. Algorand comes second with five pluses, followed by Neo with three, even though the latter allows for a shorter implementation of the supply chain than the former. Cardano and EOS required the most effort, with markedly more issues than the other platforms. Smart contracts on EOS tend to be longer than those on other platforms.

Table 4. Implementation Effort for the Use Cases

Platform	Token				NFT				Supply Chain			
	LOC	time	XP	issues	LOC	time	XP	issues	LOC	time	XP	issues
Algorand	○	+	+	○	○	+	+	○	−	○	○	+
Cardano	+	○	+	○	+	○	○	−	−	○	○	−
EOS	○	○	○	−	−	○	○	−	−	○	○	−
Ethereum	+	+	○	+	+	+	○	+	○	+	○	+
Neo	+	+	○	○	○	+	○	○	○	○	○	○

6 Evaluation Based on the Catalog of Criteria

In this section, we evaluate the five platforms according to the criteria introduced in Sect. 2. The discussion is based on the following sources: Algorand [15,28], Cardano [29], EOS [22,26,30–34], Ethereum [25,35,36], and NEO [37–40].

6.1 Technological Aspects

Table 5 lists the technological aspects.

Table 5. Platform Comparison - Technological Aspects

Criterion	Algorand	Cardano	EOS	Ethereum	Neo
Objectives	fast, secure dApps	secure, sustainable dApps	scalable, flexible dApps	general dApps	digital assets
Origin, Organisation	2019, Foundation	2017, IOHK	2018, Block.one	2015, Foundation	2016, OnChain + Foundation
Governance	algorithm, stakeholder voting	stakeholders	community voting, referendums	community, core developers	community proposals, foundation
Consensus	pure PoS	PoS	delegated PoS	PoS	delegated BFT
Interoperability	integrated atomic swaps	(plans for) cross-chain communication protocols	Inter-Blockchain Communication Protocol	on Layer 2	(plans for) NeoX

Objectives: All blockchains are general purpose platforms and aim for decentralized application (dApps). Neo puts an explicit focus on digital assets. Algorand and EOS emphasize scalability, Algorand and Cardano also security.

Origin and Organization: Ethereum went online in 2015, with Neo, Cardano, EOS, and Algorand following, in this order, on an annual basis. All platforms are backed by a foundation and/or a company.

Governance [1]: While Algorand and Cardano are governed by the stakeholders, EOS, Ethereum and Neo are open to the community to varying degrees. For decisions, EOS holds referendums, Ethereum involves the core developers, and Neo its foundation.

Consensus [21]: All platforms have similar consensus mechanisms in place, namely variants of proof-of-stake (PoS).

Interoperability [4, 16]: Algorand and EOS integrate protocols for inter-operating with other platforms, Cardano and Neo have plans to follow suit. Ethereum realizes interoperability through layer 2 solutions.

6.2   Development Aspects

Tables 6 and 7 list the development aspects.

Table 6. Platform Comparison - Development Aspects - Part 1

Criterion	Algorand	Cardano	EOS	Ethereum	Neo
Chains	mainnet, test: pPoS (2)	mainnet, test: PoS (3)	mainnet, test: dPoS (4)	mainnet, test: PoS (1), PoA (2)	mainnet, test: dBFT (1)
Permission	all 3	all 3	all 3 (on top of public)	all 3	all 3
Setup	multiple ways easy	multiple ways easy	multiple ways easy	multiple ways easy	multiple ways easy
Languages	Python/PyTeal; Java, JavaScript, Go	Marlowe, Plutus; Aiken, Opshin	C++, WebAssembly; Javascript, Java, Swift	Solidity, Vyper; Yul, Yul+, FE	Java, C#; Go, Python, JavaScript
Documen-tation	extensive, structured	extensive, but basic, less structured	detailed	rich, well organized	basic

Chains: All platforms provide a mainnet and one or more test nets.

Permission Type: All platforms can be used as public, private or consortium blockchains. In EOS, the non-public versions are built on top of the public mainnet.

Local Setup: For all platforms, the local setup can be done in multiple ways and is easy to accomplish.

Language Support: Ethereum and Cardano rely on programming languages designed specifically for smart contracts. Algorand recommends to use Python with the library PyTeal, but also provides SDKs for a few other common languages, like EOS and Neo do.

Documentation: We determine the quality of the available documentation depending on whether it covers (1) basic concepts, (2) the technology stack, (3) development basics, and (4) advanced topics.

Algorand provides an extensive, well structured documentation to the point that it is almost too much. Cardano provides good basic documentation for development albeit with little structure, while the advanced topics miss practical aspects. The documentation of EOS is detailed, but offers only few examples and hardly any advanced material. Ethereum's documentation is rich and well organized in all regards. Neo offers rather basic documentation with little introductory and advanced material.

Table 7. Platform Comparison - Development Aspects - Part 2

Criterion	Algorand	Cardano	EOS	Ethereum	Neo
2cm Developer community	medium	small	small	very large	medium
	70 k	1 k	10 k	millions	100 k
	highly responsive	responsive	responsive	very responsive	unresponsive
Sample code	many	few	few	many	few
Tutorials	many	few	several	many	few
Tools, Testing	many	several	several	many	several
	mature	mature	mature	mature	mature
Standards	few	many	few	many	several
	built-in	process	process	process	process

Community: The size of the developer communities and their willingness to support others vary greatly between the platforms. The platforms have dedicated community sections on their websites, showcasing various ways to get involved. While Ethereum has by far the largest developer community, the ones of Algorand or Neo are also fairly large. Those of Cardano and EOS are quite small (up to a few thousand).[4] All communities are responsive to development questions except for Neo's, which was to be unresponsive to questions in English.

Sample Code: Being able to start contract development from sample code is invaluable [27]. Still, not all platform seem to acknowledge its importance.

While Algorand and Ethereum provide code samples for numerous use cases, the others offer just a few examples.

Tutorials: Regarding easy access to learning materials, the picture is similar to the sample code. Although important for onboarding, Cardano and Neo provide just a few tutorials, and EOS slightly more. In contrast, Algorand and Ethereum provide a sufficient number of tutorials.

Tools and Testing: Tools play a critical role in developing smart contracts by simplifying and automating the processes [5, 27]. Smart contracts are inherently complex, and programming them can be a daunting task for even the most experienced developers. Utilizing appropriate tools, such as integrated development environments (IDEs), testing frameworks, and deployment platforms, can significantly enhance a developer's efficiency, accuracy, and overall productivity.

Again, the number of tools for Algorand and Ethereum stands out, while the other platform offer less tools to support developers.

Standards: The platforms differ in the number of standards available and in the processes for releasing new ones. While Algorand only provides a built-in standard for different kinds of assets, the other platform have established processes for adopting improvement proposals including standards. Cardano and Ethereum offer many standards, whereas Algorand and EOS have only a few.

---

[4] The numbers are based on estimates of the member counts of developer channels and forums like Reddit, Discord, Stack Exchange, Stack Overflow, and Telegram. There is an unclear overlap of channels where developers communicate.

7   Discussion

7.1   Differences to Conventional Development

An important aspect of smart contracts is that they often handle valuable assets in a decentralized setting. The following issues characterize the development of reliable smart contracts [12, 27].

- *Security.* Adversarial thinking is indispensable when developing smart contracts as they operate in a hostile environment.
- *Specification.* A full specification of the program behavior that considers all possible states and transitions would be desirable since underspecification readily leads to vulnerabilities.
- *Unpredictable and unfair scheduling.* Smart contracts are small programs activated by external events. The order of these events depends on incidental factors like the state of the network, but also on deliberate actions by network nodes that maximize their profit rather than ensure fairness. Therefore, smart contacts have to be developed with race conditions in mind.
- *Balanced Incentives.* The order of events is influenced by the incentive model of the underlying blockchain, but also by application-specific incentives implemented by the smart contracts. Programmers have to be aware of the effect of incentives and may have to balance them in order to obtain the desired behavior.
- *Novelty.* Smart contract platforms and their programming languages are still evolving. Thus, the support tools are developed for a moving target, and best practice and coding patterns emerge only gradually.

7.2   Related Work

In academia, in-depth comparisons of platforms often focus on a small number of blockchains that they compare to Ethereum [2, 11, 15, 17, 22, 23]. The respective authors employ criteria like transaction speed, execution cost, and performance [3, 6, 11, 15, 17, 22, 23] or interviews [18].

Criteria, perspectives, and use cases in related work. Valenta et al. [23] analyze differences between Ethereum, Hyperledger Fabric and Corda based on criteria like governance, mode of operation, and consensus.

EOS is a platform that tackles Ethereum's scaling issues. Song et al. [22] examine transaction data of the EOS blockchain and analyze the data of Ethereum and EOS chains from the perspective of network complexity. Dernayka et al. [11] evaluate the performance of EOS and Ethereum by triggering and measuring basic operations of a decentralized application developed specifically for this purpose. They simulate a network of 150 nodes and measure response times, CPU load and memory usage. They find that EOS.IO fails to outperform Ethereum. This observation is relevant as scalability is cited as one of the design goals of EOS, which does not seem to hold in general.

Gilad et al. [15] compare the performance of two platforms and confirm that Algorand's claim of scalability seems to hold to some extent.

Mogavero et al. [17] compare Algorand to Ethereum. One of the objectives is to measure costs and computations on blockchains by observing computational effectiveness, as it may be related to scalability. The analysis uses auctions as use case [15]. They find that "... Algorand can often be the right choice as long as decentralized computations consist of basic operations only. Instead, Ethereum is advisable when more sophisticated computations are required, in particular when ad-hoc cryptographic tasks are essential, and one can afford the involved costs and latency." These findings are in line with ours.

Mokdad et al. [18] compare three platforms and note that "the Ethereum blockchain smart contract exceeds the others in terms of development tools, resources, and community support. EOS blockchain smart contracts have the best execution speeds, and transaction costs." Regarding the development aspects of the comparison, Ethereum's superiority to EOS with respect to tools, resources, and community is in line with our findings.

Based on a systematic literature review, Bareis et al. [2] compile a catalog of criteria and compare Ethereum and NEO. It consists of the main categories Project, Blockchain Properties, Platform and Development, as well as Execution and Operation, divided into further sub-categories. As this catalog comprises many of the relevant categories, we base our own collection of criteria on it.

Our work. Our work differs in the number of platforms considered as well as in the main objective. With three use cases implemented on five platforms, we concentrate on the development cycle of applications. This adds a novel dimension, as we focus on the relative effort of developing smart contracts.

7.3   Summary of Evaluation per Platform

Algorand is a platform with high throughput, fast transaction finality, and low fees. Algorand's smart contract language Python (with the library PyTeal) is easy to use, making it accessible to developers with little blockchain experience. Algorand also offers a wealth of resources for developers, including SDKs, APIs, and an online developer portal. These factors contributed to Algorand being the second best platform regarding the implementation of our three use cases.

Cardano offers significant advantages in scalability and transaction throughput. Its smart contract language, Plutus, is based on the functional programming language Haskell. Cardano has extensive, but less structured documentation. Developer support is available through its educational portal, Plutus Playground, but limited regarding the size of the community, sample code, and tutorials. This made Cardano one of the more difficult platforms for our use cases. In fact, we were not able to fully implement the supply chain within the allotted time.

EOS uses a unique delegated proof-of-stake (dPoS) consensus mechanism that allows for high transaction throughput and low latency. Its smart contract language, C++, is widely used and offers a high degree of flexibility. EOS has an active developer community. It offers some resources and support through its online forums and documentation. Overall, it EOS turned out to be the most difficult platform, with the highest number of issues and the contracts being longer than for the other platforms.

Ethereum has a large and active community, making it easy to find resources and support. It offers comprehensive development and testing tools, tutorials and sample code. For the use cases, Ethereum was the easiest to use, with the least effort required. However, the high gas fees and slow transaction times explain the popularity of layer 2 protocols for Ethereum.

Neo is a smart contract platform with a variety of programming languages, including C#, Java, and Python. With its short transaction times and low fees, it represents an attractive option for businesses. Neo also offers some developer resources, including an online developer center and documentation, albeit with just a few code samples and tutorials. The platform is based in China, which may explain why its community is unresponsive to requests in English.

8   Conclusion

We performed a structured comparison of smart contract platforms aspects based on a catalog of criteria and implementations metrics with a particular focus on development. Our work confirms that Ethereum is by far the most mature platform with the largest development community. But the other platforms also have their advantages: Cardano – scalability, Algorand – simplicity, EOS – high throughput and flexibility through C++, and Neo – multi-language support and fast transaction times.

Regarding the implementation of the three use-cases, we can summarize: While the lines of code and the time spent were lowest with Ethereum, EOS proved to be the hardest. Cardano is a special case, as the tokens were easy to implement, while the supply chain could not be realized within the time frame of 30 h. Regarding the resolution of issues, the community and documentation of Ethereum was most helpful, while EOS was most difficult (and to some extent also Cardano). However, the experience needed to implement the use cases was lowest for Algorand (and regarding tokens also for Cardano). With respect to use cases beyond tokens, Ethereum is still the main development platform, with Algorand as a serious alternative.

Even though the longevity of a platform may seem like a safe choice, our analysis has shown that this is not always the case. Our study shows that a platform's adoption is critically important since an active, responsive community can offer substantial support. It increases the likelihood that many different use-cases have yet been implemented, or that common issues, such as those related to syntax, standards, and compilers, have already been addressed and solved. We can conclude that the choice of platform depends foremost on the requirements of the use case (standard solutions do not require much support), then on the team competence (experienced teams need less support, but may also tackle more difficult applications), and lastly on time constraints.

Limitations and further work *Platforms*: The selection of platforms was based on current trends. In a rapidly evolving domain like blockchains where new platforms are emerging, and the popularity and adoption of platforms is changing, regular evaluations are necessary. *Use cases*: We have focused on a few popular use cases. Further studies could expand the range of use cases.

References

1. Allen, D.W., Berg, C.: Blockchain governance: what we can learn from the economics of corporate governance. J. British Blockchain Assoc. **3**(1) (2020). https://doi.org/10.31585/jbba-3-1-(8)2020
2. Bareis, M., Di Angelo, M., Salzer, G.: Functional differences of Neo and Ethereum as smart contract platforms. In: 2nd International Congress on Blockchain and Applications (ICBA). Springer (2020). https://doi.org/10.1007/978-3-030-52535-4_2
3. Benahmed, S., et al.: A comparative analysis of distributed ledger technologies for smart contract development. In: 2019 IEEE 30th Annual International Symposium on Personal, Indoor and Mobile Radio Communications (PIMRC), pp. 1–6 (2019). https://doi.org/10.1109/PIMRC.2019.8904256
4. Bishnoi, M., Bhatia, R.: Interoperability solutions for blockchain. In: 2020 International Conference on Smart Technologies in Computing, Electrical and Electronics (ICSTCEE), pp. 381–385 (2020). https://doi.org/10.1109/ICSTCEE49637.2020.9277054
5. Bosu, A., Iqbal, A., Shahriyar, R., Chakraborty, P.: Understanding the motivations, challenges and needs of blockchain software developers: a survey. Empirical Softw. Eng. **24**(4), 2636–2673 (2019). https://doi.org/10.1007/s10664-019-09708-7
6. Capocasale, V., Gotta, D., Perboli, G.: Comparative analysis of permissioned blockchain frameworks for industrial applications. Blockchain: Res. Appl. **4**(1) (2023). https://doi.org/10.1016/j.bcra.2022.100113
7. Chang, S.E., Chen, Y.: When blockchain meets supply chain: a systematic literature review on current development and potential applications. IEEE Access **8**, 62478–62494 (2020). https://doi.org/10.1109/ACCESS.2020.2983601
8. Chen, Y.: Blockchain tokens and the potential democratization of entrepreneurship and innovation. Bus. Horiz. **61**(4), 567–575 (2018). https://doi.org/10.1016/j.bushor.2018.03.006
9. Chohan, R., Paschen, J.: NFT marketing: how marketers can use nonfungible tokens in their campaigns. Bus. Horiz. (2021). https://doi.org/10.1016/j.bushor.2021.12.004
10. Dabbene, F., Gay, P., Tortia, C.: Traceability issues in food supply chain management: a review. Biosyst. Eng. **120**, 65–80 (2014). https://doi.org/10.1016/j.biosystemseng.2013.09.006, operations Management in Bio-production Systems
11. Dernayka, I., Chehab, A.: Blockchain development platforms: performance comparison. In: 2021 11th IFIP International Conference on New Technologies, Mobility and Security (NTMS), pp. 1–6 (2021). https://doi.org/10.1109/NTMS49979.2021.9432669
12. Di Angelo, M., Sack, C., Salzer, G.: SoK: development of secure smart contracts - lessons from a graduate course. In: 3rd Workshop on Trusted Smart Contracts, Financial Cryptography 2019, Proceedings, pp. 91–105. Springer, LNCS 11599 (2020). https://doi.org/10.1007/978-3-030-43725-1_8
13. di Angelo, M., Salzer, G.: Identification of token contracts on Ethereum: standard compliance and beyond. Int. J. Data Sci. Anal. (2021). https://doi.org/10.1007/s41060-021-00281-1

14. Dias, L.S., Ierapetritou, M.G.: From process control to supply chain management: an overview of integrated decision making strategies. Comput. Chem. Eng. **106**, 826–835 (2017). https://doi.org/10.1016/j.compchemeng.2017.02.006, eSCAPE-26

15. Gilad, Y., Hemo, R., Micali, S., Vlachos, G., Zeldovich, N.: Algorand: scaling byzantine agreements for cryptocurrencies. In: Proceedings of the 26th Symposium on Operating Systems Principles, pp. 51–68. SOSP '17, Association for Computing Machinery, New York, NY, USA (2017). https://doi.org/10.1145/3132747.3132757

16. Koens, T., Poll, E.: Assessing interoperability solutions for distributed ledgers. Pervasive Mobile Comput. **59**, 101079 (2019). https://www.sciencedirect.com/science/article/pii/S1574119218306266

17. Mogavero, F., Visconti, I., Vitaletti, A., Zecchini, M.: The blockchain quadrilemma: when also computational effectiveness matters. In: 2021 IEEE Symposium on Computers and Communications (ISCC), pp. 1–6 (2021). https://doi.org/10.1109/ISCC53001.2021.9631511

18. Mokdad, I., Hewahi, N.M.: Empirical evaluation of blockchain smart contracts. In: Khan, M.A., Quasim, M.T., Algarni, F., Alharthi, A. (eds.) Decentralised Internet of Things. SBD, vol. 71, pp. 45–71. Springer, Cham (2020). https://doi.org/10.1007/978-3-030-38677-1_3

19. Rejeb, A., Keogh, J.G., Treiblmaier, H.: Leveraging the internet of things and blockchain technology in supply chain management. Future Internet **11**(7) (2019). https://www.mdpi.com/1999-5903/11/7/161

20. Saberi, S., Kouhizadeh, M., Sarkis, J., Shen, L.: Blockchain technology and its relationships to sustainable supply chain management. Int. J. Prod. Res. **57**(7), 2117–2135 (2019). https://doi.org/10.1080/00207543.2018.1533261

21. Sankar, L.S., Sindhu, M., Sethumadhavan, M.: Survey of consensus protocols on blockchain applications. In: 2017 4th International Conference on Advanced Computing and Communication Systems (ICACCS), pp. 1–5 (2017). https://doi.org/10.1109/ICACCS.2017.8014672

22. Song, W., et al.: EOS.IO blockchain data analysis. J. Supercomput. **78**, 5974–6005 (2021). https://doi.org/10.1007/s11227-021-04090-y

23. Valenta, M., Sandner, P.: Comparison of Ethereum, Hyperledger Fabric and Corda. Tech. rep., Frankfurt School, Blockchain Center (2017). https://www.smallake.kr/wp-content/uploads/2017/07/2017_Comparison-of-Ethereum-Hyperledger-Corda.pdf

24. Voloder, A.: Comparison of Smart Contract Platforms for Decentralized Applications Development. Master's thesis, TU Wien, Vienna, Austria (2023)

25. Wood, G., et al.: Ethereum: a secure decentralised generalised transaction ledger (2014). https://ethereum.github.io/yellowpaper/paper.pdf

26. Xu, B., Luthra, D., Cole, Z., Blakely, N.: EOS: an architectural, performance, and economic analysis (2018). https://blog.bitmex.com/wp-content/uploads/2018/11/eos-test-report.pdf

27. Zou, W., et al.: Smart contract development: challenges and opportunities. IEEE Trans. Softw. Eng. **47**(10), 2084–2106 (2021). https://doi.org/10.1109/TSE.2019.2942301

28. Algorand developer docs. https://developer.algorand.org/docs/. Accessed 15 Apr 2023

29. Cardano developer docs. https://docs.cardano.org/cardano-testnet/getting-started. Accessed 29 Apr 2023

30. Eos network documentation. https://docs.eosnetwork.com/docs/latest/smart-contracts/getting-started/dune-guide/. Accessed 01 Apr 2023

31. EOS reference smart contracts. https://github.com/EOSIO/eosio.contracts. Accessed 29 Mar 2023
32. EOSIO documentation. https://developers.eos.io/manuals/eos/v2.0/nodeos/usage/development-environment/index. Accessed 07 Mar 2023
33. EOSIO official documentation. https://developers.eos.io/welcome/latest/manuals/index. Accessed 27 Mar 2023
34. EOSIO public blockchain documentation. https://eos.io/eos-public-blockchain/. Accessed 07 Mar 2023
35. Ethereum development documentation. https://ethereum.org/en/developers/docs/. Accessed 06 Jan 2023
36. Ethereum development tutorials. https://ethereum.org/en/developers/tutorials/. Accessed 24 Feb 2023
37. Neo development documentation. https://docs.neo.org/docs/en-us/develop/network/testnet.html. Accessed 06 Jan 2023
38. Neo development examples. https://neo.org/dev#examples. Accessed 23 Feb 2023
39. Neo-express documentation. https://github.com/neo-project/neo-express. Accessed 16 Jan 2023
40. Neo whitepaper. https://docs.neo.org/v2/docs/en-us/basic/whitepaper.html. Accessed 06 Jan 2023

Framework for Design and Development of Blockchain Applications Using Smart Contracts

Sumati Kulkarni, Joseph Wireman^(✉), and Nasseh Tabrizi

East Carolina University, Greenville, NC 27858, USA
Wiremanj20@students.ecu.edu

Abstract. Blockchain technology is generating a lot of buzz due to its potential to disrupt many existing industries and business processes. Blockchain technology, which was first developed as part of Bitcoin's underlying infrastructure, provides a framework for decentralized and transparent transaction management amongst untrustworthy parties. Many people feel that this blockchain component would alter existing supply chain processes, which often include many untrustworthy organizations, from raw material extraction to the ultimate consumption of a finished product by the end customer. While numerous claims have been made about its apparent benefits in supply chain management, there have only been a few technological applications established that are beneficial in real-world circumstances. A smart contract is a computer protocol that digitally enables, validates, and enforces contract fulfillment utilizing Blockchain technology. Because smart contracts are trackable and irreversible and enable the performance of credible transactions without the involvement of third parties, they can be used to effectively replace existing supply chain mechanisms. In this paper, we present a system for facilitating the sale of products between untrustworthy organizations using smart contract technology to replace the "letter of credit" payment mechanism effectively. An innovative dispute resolution method is created, and decentralized software is built and deployed on the Ethereum blockchain using Solidity smart contracts. We've demonstrated how to create a revolutionary public decentralized application that may take the place of well-established conventional instruments like letters of credit using just tools that are open source. We also create a dispute resolution algorithm that, in theory, outperforms other accessible online conflict settlement tools.

Keywords: Framework · Blockchain · Smart contracts

1 Introduction

Blockchain technology provides a novel platform for decentralized and transparent transaction processing, it was created in 2008 as part of Bitcoin's underlying technology [1]. Blockchain creates a digital ledger using a decentralized, peer-to-peer network to create a continuous, expanding collection of ordered information called blocks. The network

Q. Wang et al. (Eds.): ICBC 2023, LNCS 14206, pp. 119–131, 2023.
https://doi.org/10.1007/978-3-031-44920-8_8

then validates each transaction, represented in a cryptographically signed block. Despite early reservations about this technology, governments, and big organizations have lately researched ways to adapt and develop it in various applications, ranging from banking, social, and legal industries to designing manufacturing and supply chain networks. At the same time, scholars are debating the feasibility of using Blockchain technology to tackle real-world problems.

We will discuss some of the terminology and essential ideas of supply chain management to offer some context for why it is being explored as a possible application area for blockchain technology. SCM is defined as the active management of supply chain operations to optimize customer value and gain a long-term competitive advantage. The transportation and storage of raw materials, work-in-process inventories, and finished items from the point of origin to the end of consumption is part of managing the flow of commodities and services in commerce [2]. Organizations increasingly rely on effective supply chains or networks to compete in the global market and networked economy. This idea of business partnerships extends beyond traditional organizational boundaries in new management paradigms [3] and tries to arrange complete business operations across a value chain of several organizations. With intricate interactions among participants, however, mistrust amongst players becomes a self-fulfilling prophecy, resulting in a lack of visibility/transparency and, eventually, a reduction in the value offered to consumers. Improving trust and visibility across a supply chain has benefited all parties involved.

By enabling reliable, accurate information exchange across numerous parties without trust, blockchain technology can solve a fundamental facet of the supply chain. Blockchain technology can solve a fundamental facet of the supply chain by enabling reliable, accurate information exchange across numerous parties without trust. This can also reduce the need for many "middlemen" who are now utilized to facilitate transactions between untrustworthy parties. An example of this would be when importing high-value commodities from a distant source.

Due to a lack of trust between the two parties, it is usual practice to enlist the help of a financial institution, such as a bank, to mediate the purchase of items and the transfer of money. For a nominal charge, the bank will ensure that a cash transfer occurs only after the physical handover of items. A blockchain application may efficiently handle this process by ensuring cash release only after receiving proof of shipping from the provider. This paper will further investigate different uses of this type in this thesis to uncover suitable use cases that may transform into real-world blockchain applications. The following are the goals of this paper:

- Conduct blockchain mapping research as it relates to supply chain management.
- Develop a framework for a blockchain-based letter of credit that overcomes issues with current methods.
- Systematic technological review to determine the optimal set of tools.
- Create a unique method for resolving disputes while smart contracts are being executed.
- Create a web application to evaluate the framework's efficacy.

2 Development of Blockchain Applications

2.1 Proof of Concept

Consider huge merchants such as Amazon or Walmart: consumers send payments first, and the provider ships the goods afterward. It is also fairly commonplace for cash to be sent after the delivery of a product, particularly in B2B (Business-to-Business) trans-actions. In other words, either the buyer or the seller must have faith in the other party and transfer products or monies with the expectation that the other party will fulfill their half of the bargain. While there is always legal redress if one of the parties fails to act under the initial agreement, it may be challenging to enforce legality across international borders. When a product is exclusively accessible from a single source and outside of the country's borders, purchasers risk losing their money with no legal remedy. In the sellers' case, this might very quickly happen if they are selling to unknown buyers outside their nation and expecting payment after the delivery of products. Financial institutions, such as banks, have an instrument to trade products and monies while absolving both parties of any risk involved with the transfer to assist both parties in this case. This instrument is known as a "Letter of Credit."

Letter of Credit
A letter of credit, sometimes known as a "credit letter," is a document issued by a bank guaranteeing that a buyer's payment to a seller will be paid on time and in full. If the buyer cannot make a payment on the purchase, the bank will cover the entire or remaining sum [4]. The flow in the supply chain is presented in Fig. 1.

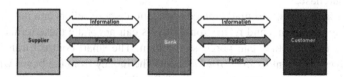

Fig. 1. Flow in the supply chain with Letter-of-credit

The bank now acts as an intermediary, ensuring that funds are transferred from the customer to the supplier only after the goods are delivered as agreed. While this technique allows transactions between two mutually distrusting parties, the bank imposes a fee beginning at 0.75% of the purchase price. In the case of high-priced commodities, these fees quickly pile up, increasing supply chain costs and decreasing the total supply chain surplus. Adding an intermediary also lengthens the time it takes to execute a transaction by introducing extra touchpoints and handshakes into the process. Such transactions would be ideal for a permissionless blockchain application since all parties are unknown at the outset, and transparency/public verifiability is required to avoid fraudulent activity.

Proof of Concept: Decentralized Letter of Credit
We suggest a decentralized marketplace application in this part that can effectively replace a letter of credit. Assume that a customer wants to acquire a certain item from

an unknown vendor. For simplicity, we'll assume there are no product returns or partial shipments/refunds. After successfully getting the item, the customer gets reimbursed the whole amount or pays the full amount. While numerous supply chain issues can be inspected from the time an item is purchased by the buyer to the time the seller receives payment, we only consider the following four cases (Table 1) in which either the buyer or the seller is fraudulent and provide provisions within the decentralized app to efficiently resolve these.

Table 1. Potential outcomes with decentralized purchasing.

Potential outcomes after purchase		Seller	
		Good	Bad
Buyer	Good	Seller ships item, buyer confirms receipt, and seller receives payments.	Seller doesn't ship/ships wrong/defective item and still receives payment from buyer.
	Bad	Seller ships item, but buyer does not confirm receipt an does not release payments.	When both parties are fraudulent there's no transaction. Seller doesn't ship and buyer doesn't pay.

The Decentralized Software must address scenarios when either one or both actors are fraudulent, as when both are fraudulent, there is no issue to be solved. As a result, the smart contract-based dApp should be able to pay excellent vendors even if the customer does not acknowledge receipt of the goods. Furthermore, dApp should be able to repay a genuine customer if they have yet to get an item as promised from a dishonest vendor. We assume that the buyer and seller will agree on all specifics of expected delivery before the purchase.

We offer a decentralized marketplace application where sellers can put their things for sale along with terms and restrictions. Buyers can negotiate these terms, and if an agreement is reached, they can purchase the item. The smart contract transfers Ether from the buyer's account to an escrow account. The money from the buyer will be kept here until the transfer is completed successfully. This also sends a notification to the Seller, requesting that they dispatch the item. When the consumer receives the products as intended, they may 'confirm receipt,' enabling the smart contract to disburse payments and record the transaction in a new block. The proof of concept of the decentralized letter of credit application is depicted in Fig. 2.

Consider the following scenarios: the buyer fails to acknowledge receipt after getting an item specified in the purchase agreement. If the buyer fails to confirm within the agreed-upon number of days, the marketplace website will provide the seller the opportunity to 'challenge the transaction.' When a seller wants a dispute resolution, the transaction is shared with ADMINs, who can serve as jurors. These ADMINs may then examine all of the papers given by the seller during the time frame specified, as well as prior transactions of buyers and sellers, to determine whether the buyer or seller is operating fraudulently. At the end of the time limit, all the ADMINs are tallied to decide whether the buyer should be reimbursed, or the seller should be compensated. When the smart contract receives the judgment from ADMINs, it will either reimburse the buyer or execute payment to the seller, and the transaction will be recorded on the blockchain.

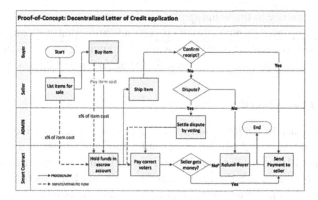

Fig. 2. Proof-of-concept of decentralized letter of credit application

To guarantee that ADMINs perform as excellent jurors and do not vote arbitrarily, only those who voted for the majority group will be compensated for their time on the jury.

Furthermore, the charge for resolving a disagreement is deducted straight from the account of the buyer or seller. This inhibits fraudulent conduct and encourages parties to address small disagreements offline rather than creating arguments.

As this smart contract spreads and many ADMINs are available to settle disputes, ADMINs may be given even better access to voting on transactions involving more significant sums of money based on their track record of adequately identifying the party with the majority of votes. This will have the twin effect of motivating ADMINs to vote carefully while simultaneously punishing ADMINs who vote arbitrarily to obtain a dispute resolution fee.

The number of transactions on which ADMINs can vote can also be time-phased so that no one ADMIN can cast multiple votes in a short period. Lastly, each transaction can have a max number of votes that decays over time upon reaching which the choice will be determined and a new transaction posted to the blockchain.

3 Design and Development of Decentralized Applications Using Solidity Smart Contracts

3.1 Requirements

To create a decentralized application (dApp) that can successfully replace a standard letter of credit, we would require a website that serves as a marketplace for buyers and sellers. Sellers must be able to offer their things for sale here, and buyers must be able to purchase using Ether, which the smart contract must hold until the transaction is completed. Once the item is delivered/service is given, the buyer must be able to acknowledge receipt of goods/services, which should cause the smart contract to pay the seller. If the buyer does not confirm receipt within a predetermined number of days, the seller should be able to open a dispute and attach the relevant documentation. This issue must then be broadcast to admin accounts, which function as jurors and vote to decide the dispute in favor of either the buyer or seller. The contract must then be able to transmit money to the winning party and pay the administrators who voted for the majority group as a dispute resolution fee, indicating that the contract has been completed. If neither party takes any action after the purchase for an extended time, the buyer shall be reimbursed for the sum paid for the acquisition of the goods/service.

3.2 Proposed Framework

To achieve these needs, we may utilize the Truffle suite, which provides a framework with all of the resources needed for the creation and deployment of a dApp bundled and ready-to-go. Metamask may be used to conduct digital currency transactions. The smart contract is created in Solidity and tested in the remix IDE. The front end may be constructed with Angular JS and Web3, both of which are supported by Truffle Suite. Any supported database, such as MongoDB or SQLite, may be used to create a backend for offline transaction processing. Finally, the smart contract may be created and deployed using Ganache, a platform that simulates blockchain networks on local machines [5]. We might install the smart contract on the Sepolia Ethereum test network for testing and quality assurance, a real-time blockchain for testing new apps [6]. Once the smart contracts have been tested and approved, they may be deployed on the Ethereum main network.

Unknown parties would likely use a decentralized letter of credit application as envisioned in this section. Because none of them can be trusted, doing this work in a permissioned blockchain such as Hyperledger would be difficult. This type of blockchain network is better suited for enterprise-level implementations in which all players are recognized and trusted. The application envisioned here would be installed directly on the blockchain and must be available globally.

While Hyperledger provides excellent performance scalability. Because letters of credit are typically requested for high-value goods/services that cannot be supplied quickly, the application should see a low volume of transactions. Furthermore, normal lead times for such goods/times might range from weeks to months. In such instances, a few minutes or even hours of transaction time would be insignificant. Transaction fees are also unimportant since the number of transactions for every participant would be limited, and the individual transaction values would be significant. A greater transaction charge may even be beneficial since it discourages low-value commodity merchants from clogging network capacity. For such an application, security, dependability, and an audit record of transactions are critical. Finally, because smart contract logic may quickly become intricate with changing business circumstances, the platform on which it is installed must be turning complete.

Considering the characteristics and ramifications discussed in Section II, we continue to create our decentralized letter of a credit application on Ethereum, utilizing the Solidity language for constructing smart contracts. Even with a fee for dispute resolution, the overall cost of a transaction would be significantly lower than going via a central agency such as a bank. Furthermore, when there is no disagreement, neither the buyer nor the seller incurs any costs other than the minor transaction fee, which is negligible in comparison to the cost of the goods/service and the benefit it provides to both parties.

3.3 Metamask, Truffle Suite and Ganache

MetaMask is a browser plugin that allows users to manage accounts and keys in several ways while keeping them separate from the site environment [7]. This significantly enhances security because keeping user keys on a single central server, or even locally, might lead to mass account thefts. Furthermore, this plugin allows developers to communicate with the globally available Ethereum API, which recognizes users of web3-compatible browsers. Anytime a transaction signature is required, MetaMask notifies users of the transactions. MetaMask aids in retrieving data from the blockchain and allows users to securely sign and manage blockchain transactions. MetaMask supports many networks, including the Ethereum main network, infura's Ethereum test networks, and Ganache's local blockchain network.

Tim Coulter invented Truffle Suite, a platform for developing, testing, and deploying applications on the Ethereum network [5]. Truffle, Ganache, and Drizzle are the three core development frameworks for Ethereum smart contract and dApp development that comprise the Truffle Framework [8].

Truffle is a programming environment, testing framework, and deployment pipeline for Ethereum decentralized applications (dApps). Truffle handles contract artifact management and offers support for bespoke deployments, library linking, and complicated Ethereum applications. It also offers automated contract testing in both JavaScript and Solidity. Finally, Truffle has an interactive console with access to all Truffle commands and contracts.

A blockchain on which these contracts will be deployed must be chosen. This might be the mainnet, a test net, or a local private blockchain called Ganache, also supplied by Truffle Suite. Truffle and Ganache work together to create a blockchain on a local workstation for testing and deploying smart contracts.

3.4 Ethereum Environment Setup

To install smart contracts on an Ethereum blockchain, we may use truffleconfig.js in the root directory to connect to it. This file provides a development network already set up for localhost by default. This configuration file may be expanded to accommodate other networks, such as a live mainnet.

Ganache provides a graphical user interface for viewing blockchain status. Ten accounts are generated upon blockchain instantiation to help with development and testing. This blockchain has no link to real-world public Ethereum blockchains. It is issued a random network ID. A mnemonic is also produced to uniquely identify this blockchain, which is instantiated automatically and accessible through localhost:8545. Within the options area, you may set up the network. By default, Ganache accelerates blockchain transactions by automatically mining blocks and processing transactions in real-time. Truffle is pre-configured to connect with Ganache by default.

Now, to deploy contracts on the live network, we can call migrate with the --network flag: truffle migrate --network live. This allows us to define a range of networks and migrate to them as required, which is helpful while moving from testing on local blockchains to deployment on a live mainnet. Because Ethereum is a peer-to-peer network of nodes, the blockchain contains copies of all data and code. Web3.js enables us to use JSON RPC to request data from a private Ethereum node and post data to the network. It's similar to jQuery with a JSON API to read and write data to and from an internet server. Web3.js looks for a web3 provider by default, a blockchain client or light node that can handle contract communication and transact on the Ethereum blockchain.

3.5 Solidity Smart Contracts

Solidity is the programming language used to create Smart Contracts. The syntax of Solidity is comparable to that of JavaScript, which enables inheritance, libraries, and sophisticated user-defined types. Solidity is a high-level programming language used to create smart contracts. Solidity is a C++, Python, and JavaScript language combination that targets the Ethereum Virtual Machine (EVM) [9, 10].

A Solidity contract is a collection of code (functions) and data (state) stored at a specific address on the Ethereum blockchain. The smart contract's whole code is available to the public, and anybody connected to the network can call functions on the smart contract.

The pragma keyword enables certain compiler features or checks. Because a pragma directive is always local to a source file, it must be included in all files if it is to be available throughout the project. When another file is imported, the pragma from that file is not applied to the importing file. Because we are using Solidity 0.6.4 in our project, this contract file will not compile with any compiler before 0.6.4, and it will also not work with any compiler beginning with 0.7.0. The code will compile as expected because there will be no breaking changes until version 0.7.0.

3.6 Buyer and Seller Registration

We've shown how to utilize a function to validate and register new users that want to use this application.

To manage errors, Solidity employs state-reverting exceptions. An exception of this type undoes any changes done to the state in the current call and all of its sub-calls, as well as reporting an error to the caller. The assert and require convenience functions can be used to check for conditions and throw an exception if the condition is not fulfilled. The need function is used here to confirm that the user account has not previously been registered as a buyer or seller.

We can retrieve the address of the account that is calling the function with msg.sender. Solidity provides this value inside the msg global variable that also lets us retrieve other account-related values, such as current ether and other user-defined variables.

3.7 Implementation of Sale Transaction

To facilitate a sale transaction, we first let the supplier use a 'ListProduct' function and collect an upfront dispute resolution fee as a proportion of the item cost. Each product is individually recognized by the product ID 'P_ID' and keeps the seller and buyer's addresses after the customer purchases the item using the 'BuyProduct' function. Using the need statements again, we guarantee that there is enough ether available to perform transactions.

Other functionalities, similar to listing and purchasing things, are added to allow the smart contract to keep track of the product and payment when it is dispatched and delivery verified. When a product is dispatched and the customer confirms the delivery, payment must be made to the suppliers, and dispute resolution must be reimbursed to both parties. If the buyer does not acknowledge receipt of goods after receiving them, the seller may initiate a dispute.

3.8 Admin Selection and Dispute Resolution Algorithm

When a dispute is initiated, ADMINs can view this transaction, as well as the seller's remarks and proof of delivery. The ADMINs can then serve as a jury and cast their votes indicating whether they believe the seller should be paid or refunded. To guarantee that votes are not cast arbitrarily, ADMINs will be charged a nominal amount. After the disagreement is resolved, the winning party receives full payment/refund, including the dispute settlement fee, which was paid in advance as a deposit with the contract. The losing party's dispute resolution charge, together with the voting money received from each ADMIN, is then divided evenly among the ADMINs voting for the winning side. If all ADMINs voted for the same party, the total dispute settlement and voting fee received is divided and paid evenly among the ADMINs.

The success of this application is dependent on dispute resolution, which is already a key emphasis area in smart contracts. Because contract disagreements are unavoidable, various firms provide online dispute resolution services, some of which are mentioned below [11]:

- *Kleros.*

An online crowdsourced arbitrator for Ethereum smart contract dispute resolution. The Kleros approach is based on game theory and the discovery of a "Schelling point" for dispute resolution. In the absence of communication, people opt for a Schelling point (or focus point) [12]. Kleros operates by engaging random admins from across the world as jurors depending on the amount of cryptocurrency, they deposit to demonstrate their availability and interest.

- *Aragon.*

Aragon is another crowdsourced ODR platform that generates flexible human-readable agreements that parties may execute using Ethereum by depositing bitcoin collateral. A party can appeal by posting a bigger bond as the complaint progresses up the chain of command, eventually reaching the Aragon "supreme court" judges, who have a very high success rate [13].

- *Jur.io.*

In Jur, contesting parties propose resolutions along with several tokens to "stake" their ideas, similar to Kleros. Voters choose which plan to support, and a decision is made after the period specified by the parties. Voters that vote against the majority are penalized with token loss, which is intended to encourage fair voting.

One of the major flaws with these techniques is that the number of voters is pre-selected and fixed, or the period in which voters can cast their ballots is predetermined.

While charging voters a price prohibits votes from being cast without a thorough eval-uation of the evidence, it also reduces the number of voters available in the system to decide disputes. Again, there is a trade-off between the quality and the number of votes that may be acquired by adjusting the voting charge [14]. The following are some issues that need to be addressed for the proper functioning of this process:

1. Incorrect decision due to too few voters.
2. Not sufficient votes collected in time.
3. Trigger for dispute settlement. Time-bound or based on the total number of votes.

Taking this into account, we created an algorithm that automatically balances the quality and quantity of votes using a decaying function that determines the number of votes necessary to decide a disagreement. The pseudocode for this algorithm is shown in Fig. 3.:

```
after every new vote and at predefined time intervals calculate:
maxvotes = f(p,t)            {where p are transaction parameters, t is
time since dispute}
if total_votes > maxvotes then:
          if lastvote = buyer then:
                  buyer_votes = buyer_votes - 1
          else :
                  seller_votes = seller_votes - 1
          settle_dispute
       elseif total_votes == maxvotes then:
          settle_dispute
       else:
          if (vote = buyer) then
                  buyer_votes = buyer_votes + 1
          else :
                  seller_votes = seller_votes + 1
          total_votes = total_votes + 1
          if total_votes == maxvotes:
                  settle_dispute
f(p,t) is a decaying function over time that always results in an odd
number
```

Fig. 3. Pseudocode of balancing the quality and quantity of votes

The number of votes necessary to settle a disagreement is computed using trans-action parameters and broadcasted to that many ADMINs chosen at random, divided by a factor representing the historical percentage of votes obtained from the number of ADMINs chosen for voting. If all the ADMINs chosen vote and pay their voting fees, the disagreement is resolved instantly. However, because time is of importance in many of these contracts, the total number of votes necessary to decide a disagreement decreases over time if the ADMINs take their time voting. The dispute resolution at the optimal time using the algorithm is shown in Fig. 4

Given that votes cannot be reversed or amended, it is fair to anticipate that the number of votes cast will continue to rise over time. We can be certain that the algorithm will terminate since it minimizes the votes necessary to decide disputes over time. Further-more, if some votes are cast, the time required to settle a dispute will be far shorter than the maximum dispute resolution period agreed upon by both parties at the outset of the transaction. The technique described here will effectively result in an automated dispute resolution at an ideal time based on ADMIN availability and the time since the dispute was initiated.

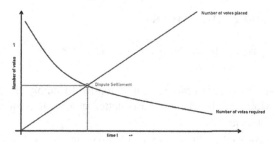

Fig. 4. Dispute resolution at the optimal time using the algorithm.

4 Evaluation

4.1 Implementation Using AngularJS

Finally, we employ AngularJS, a JavaScript-based open-source front-end web framework that aids in the creation of single-page apps for our front end [15]. After deploying the contract on a local blockchain network supplied by Ganache, the front end is launched. This website offers registration pages for new users. Adding new items and starting a dispute for the seller, confirming delivery or claiming a refund for the customer, and a dispute settlement page for the ADMINs where all disputed transactions are shown are all role-specific pages.

4.2 Result

We demonstrated how to create a disruptive public dApp utilizing open-source technologies that can replace established conventional instruments such as letters of credit. We also created a dispute resolution algorithm that, in principle, will outperform existing online conflict resolution methods. While users of this service may wind up paying a transaction cost, it will be far less than the 0.75% price imposed by the bank for a letter of credit. Because both parties profit the most when they follow through on their agreements and do not argue, this fosters ethical and professional behavior. As a result, rather than becoming the rule, conflict resolutions should become the exception. Furthermore, consumers or traders who keep their part of the contract are always insured for money deposited and are not exposed to any danger. As the network's usage develops and everyone transacts fairly, the cost of acquiring a letter of credit can be reduced to a few cents over time. Letters of credit currently cover 12.5% (1.7%) of global commerce, or $2.3 trillion ($310 billion). This massive market may be effectively harnessed through the creation and execution of this decentralized application. Finally, from an ethical standpoint, unlike several other cryptocurrency transactions or decentralized applications that provide complete anonymity, allowing illegal transactions to occur, this application would always be subject to review by the admins, who would most certainly report any illegal trade activities to the concerned agencies if they were discovered [16].

5   Conclusion and Future Works

To conclude, we have been able to achieve the objectives of this thesis outlined in Sect. 1.2 as listed below.

- Performed a mapping study of blockchain as applied to supply chain management
- Created a framework for a blockchain-based letter of credit that addresses challenges with using current techniques.
- Systematically reviewed technologies to identify best tools x Developed a novel algorithm to resolve disputes while executing smart contracts.
- Evaluated the effectiveness of this framework by creating a web application.

While we have addressed several concerns linked to the acquisition of high-value products/services in the lack of trust, many more may emerge, including but not limited to customs, change of ownership, dangerous items, force majeure events, insurance, and fraud. The principles and structure presented in this paper are intended to be a beginning in the right direction. To keep the notion simple, we leave much of the complexity to the administrators. Fortunately, we can continually expand on our smart contract and incorporate new concerns as they arise during dispute resolution. Furthermore, admins in this idea can be autonomous actors.

The success of this concept is dependent on administrators doing an excellent job of resolving conflicts. While the solution demonstrated here incentivizes admins who have regularly voted for the majority party, this system may be reinforced further by broadcasting higher-valued transactions preferentially to admins who have continuously voted for the dominant party. If an admin who has consistently voted correctly starts voting badly at any point, they should be penalized by only having voting powers on lesser-value transactions. They may boost their credibility by voting correctly and progressing to higher-value deals that will dissuade any fraudulent activity or admins working together to turn the case in favor of the buyer or seller. The number of votes necessary may be initially established depending on the value of the transaction. Still, it could gradually deteriorate to allow for dispute resolution with fewer votes as time passes. These gratifying tools would go a long way toward ensuring that disputes are resolved correctly. Furthermore, voters do not have to work against one another because administrators benefit even if all voters vote for the same party. Finally, to decrease the possibility of fraud, the admins chosen to vote might be picked randomly.

Considering that disputes can arise for various reasons and that one of the parties does not have to be at fault for each transaction. We could provide admins with the option of making a partial payment if the delivery of goods/services was not up to the buyer's expectations.

We might improve the structure of this application by allowing all blockchain players to retain voting rights via proof-of-stake. In this manner, even when there are few conflicts, all blockchain participants gain, pushing the jury to analyze the issues and vote thoroughly. As time passes, improper voting may erode trust in the program, leading to fewer transactions and use. This is not desired by blockchain stakeholders. Ultimately, this structure would encourage all parties involved to operate ethically and professionally in a genuinely decentralized and democratic manner. An Ethereum token can also be created expressly for these types of transactions and for usage with this application, which might strengthen the framework.

Finally, we believe the architecture proposed here is a unique way of designing a framework for decentralized blockchain applications. However, because we could not conduct an extensive search of current frameworks built for this purpose, it would be helpful to keep this in mind as future work.

References

1. Nakamoto, S.: A peer-to-peer electronic cash system. Bitcoin. https://bitcoin.org/bitcoin.pdf (2008)
2. Chopra, S.A.: Supply Chain Management: Strategy, Planning, and Operation. Pearson, Boston, MA (2013)
3. Drucker, P.F.: Managements new paradigms. Forbes Magazine, 98–99 (1998)
4. KAGAN, J.: Letter of credit. Retrieved from Investopedia.com (2020). https://www.invest opedia.com/terms/l/letterofcredit.asp
5. Ganache-TruffleSuite. https://trufflesuite.com/ganache/
6. Sepolia-TestnetResources. https://sepolia.dev/
7. Lee, W.-M.: Using the MetaMask chrome extension. In: Beginning Ethereum Smart Contracts Programming, pp. 93–126. Apress, Berkeley, CA (2019). https://doi.org/10.1007/978-1-4842-5086-0_5
8. Mohanty, D.: Deploying smart contracts. In: Ethereum for Architects and Developers, pp. 105–138. Apress, Berkeley, CA (2018). https://doi.org/10.1007/978-1-4842-4075-5_4
9. Dannen, C.: Introducing Ethereum and Solidity (2017)
10. Solidity-Docs. https://docs.soliditylang.org/en/v0.8.17/
11. Samaniego, M.A.: Hosting virtual IoT resources on edge-hosts with blockchain. In: 2016 IEEE International Conference on Computer and Information Technology (CIT), (pp. 116–119). IEEE (2016)
12. Smith, B.A.: IBM Blockchain: an enterprise deployment of a distributed consensus-based transaction log. In: Proceedings of the Fourth International IBM Cloud Academy Conference, pp. 140–143 (2016)
13. Aragon Dispute Resolution. https://aragon.org/aragon-court
14. Jur Review-Dispute Resolution via The Block Chain. https://coinreviews.io/jur-review/
15. Jadhav, M.A.: Single page application using Angularjs. Int. J. Comput. Sci. Inf. Technol. 2876–2879 (2015)
16. Friederike Niepmann, T.S.-E.: VOX CEPR Policy Portal. Retrieved from Trade finance around the world (2016). https://voxeu.org/article/trade-finance-around-world

Application and Industry Track

Vehicle Ownership, Leasing, and Rental Blockchain Protocol VOLR BP

Adel ELMessiry[2](✉) [ID], Magdi El Messiry[3] [ID], and Kenzy ElMessiry[1] [ID]

[1] Vanderbilt University, Nashville, USA
[2] WebDBTech, New York, USA
Adel.ElMessiry@gmail.com
[3] Alexandria University, Alexandria, Egypt

Abstract. Blockchain technology has emerged as a disruptive force in recent years, holding the potential to revolutionize various industries. One sector that stands to greatly benefit from blockchain is the automotive industry. In 2021, the global automotive market size reached USD 2.73 trillion and is projected to reach USD 3.27 trillion by 2028, exhibiting a Compound Annual Growth Rate (CAGR) of 3.01%. This article introduces a protocol called Vehicle Ownership, Leasing, and Rental Blockchain Protocol (VOLR BP), which utilizes blockchain and Non-Fungible Tokens (NFTs) to create digital replicas of vehicles. These digital twins enable the secure and transparent transfer of ownership, leasing, and rental transactions. The VOLR BP aims to address existing challenges in vehicle ownership and streamline the processes involved in vehicle leasing and rental, ultimately fostering increased trust, efficiency and decreased administrative overhead.

Keywords: Automotive · Blockchain · NFTs

1 Introduction

The global economy greatly depends on the automotive industry, as it offers transportation solutions to individuals, businesses, and various sectors [1]. Nevertheless, conventional methods of owning, leasing, and renting vehicles have suffered from inefficiencies, a lack of transparency, and trust problems. These obstacles have generated a demand for innovative solutions that can optimize operations, increase security, and enhance the overall customer journey. Over the past few years, blockchain technology has gained recognition as a promising solution that has the potential to tackle these issues effectively [2]. By offering a transparent, secure, and decentralized framework, blockchain can revolutionize the management of vehicle ownership, leasing, and rental transactions [3]. In the past, the only available method for managing waste and ensuring quality was through centralized control of the supply chain. However, with the growth of Blockchain (distributed ledger technology) [4], decentralized control became a means of improving the quality and speed of supply chains while eliminating

Q. Wang et al. (Eds.): ICBC 2023, LNCS 14206, pp. 135–146, 2023.
https://doi.org/10.1007/978-3-031-44920-8_9

waste and reducing economic costs [5]. Treiblmaier, makes the case that only Blockchain applications can satisfactorily address and improve the "triple bottom lines" of the supply chain's goals for social, economic and environmental sustainability as shown in Fig. 1.

Fig. 1. Triple bottom line goal system.

2   Challenges of Vehicle Industry

There are many issues with how vehicles are now owned [6], leased, and rented. The hazards associated with fraud, forgery, and a lack of transparency in ownership records are significant for both buyers and sellers [7]. The administrative burden and the complexity of paperwork involved in transferring ownership result in delays, errors, and higher costs [8]. In the case of leasing, trust issues emerge due to the lack of transparency in lease terms and limited flexibility for lessees. Rental services face challenges in verifying the eligibility of renters, tracking vehicle usage, and settling payments efficiently. These problems hinder the growth and efficiency of the automotive industry, necessitating a robust and reliable solution.

3   VOLR Cost Reduction

The actual cost savings and efficiencies achieved through the use of blockchain in the automotive industry can vary significantly based on various factors such as the specific use case, implementation strategy, organization size, and industry context. Nonetheless, there have been studies and reports highlighting the potential benefits of blockchain in terms of cost savings and efficiency improvements. For example, a report by IBM and the Ford Motor Company suggested that blockchain could help reduce warranty disputes and associated costs by improving the transparency and accuracy of vehicle maintenance and repair records. Another report by Accenture estimated that blockchain implementation in supply chain management within the automotive industry could potentially lead to cost savings of up to 20% by reducing paperwork, eliminating manual errors, improving inventory management, and enhancing traceability [9].

However potential cost savings are based on the reported benefits and use cases of blockchain technology [10]. Actual savings will depend on the specific implementation and circumstances. Here are a few examples:

3.1   Supply Chain Management

Implementing blockchain in the automotive supply chain can reduce costs associated with fraud, counterfeiting, and supply chain inefficiencies. According to a report by IBM [11], blockchain can potentially reduce recall costs by up to 80% through improved traceability and faster identification of faulty parts or components.

3.2   Payment Processing

The use of blockchain-based smart contracts can streamline payment processes, reduce administrative overheads, and eliminate the need for intermediaries [12]. A study by Deloitte [13] suggests that smart contracts can save companies 15–30% of processing costs compared to traditional payment systems [14].

3.3   Vehicle Lifecycle Management

Blockchain can enhance efficiency in managing vehicle lifecycle processes, including maintenance, repairs, and ownership transfers. By reducing paperwork, eliminating manual processes, and enhancing transparency, cost savings can be achieved in administrative tasks and operational efficiencies [15–17].

3.4   Data Management and Sharing

Blockchain technology can improve data sharing and management across multiple stakeholders in the automotive industry. This can lead to cost savings through reduced data reconciliation efforts, improved data integrity, and enhanced data security [1,18,19].

3.5   Fraud Prevention and Risk Mitigation

Blockchain's immutability and transparency can help prevent fraud and mitigate risks associated with the automotive industry. This can reduce costs related to insurance fraud, warranty claims, and dispute resolutions [20]. It's important to note that these examples are based on general observations and case studies from various industries. The actual cost savings will depend on the specific implementation, scale, and context of blockchain adoption in the automotive industry [21]. Conducting a thorough analysis and considering the specific use case and organizational context will provide a more accurate estimation of potential cost savings [22].

4   Proposed System

The main objectives of the Vehicle Ownership, Leasing, and Rental Blockchain Protocol (VOLR BP) are as follows:

4.1   Enhance Transparency and Trust

The protocol intends to eradicate fraud, forgery, and errors in ownership records while establishing a transparent and unchangeable ecosystem for car ownership, leasing, and renting. For all parties, the protocol offers a reliable and impenetrable platform by utilizing blockchain technology.

4.2   Streamline Processes

The protocol focuses on enhancing security methods to safeguard confidential information. The VOLR BP protects personal and financial data, lowering the likelihood of data breaches and identity theft through cryptographic methods and access control systems.

4.3   Improve Security and Data Privacy

The protocol focuses on strengthening security measures to protect sensitive data and ensure privacy. Through cryptographic techniques and access control mechanisms, VOLR BP safeguards personal and financial information, reducing the risks of data breaches and identity theft.

4.4   Foster Efficiency and Cost Savings

By minimizing paperwork, eliminating manual verification procedures, and decreasing administrative costs, VOLR BP seeks to increase operating efficiency. All parties involved-manufacturers, dealerships, lessors, lessees, and rental service providers-save money as a result of this.

4.5   Facilitate Peer-to-Peer Transactions

Peer-to-peer vehicle sharing is envisioned by the protocol, giving users the option to directly lease or rent vehicles from other owners. VOLR BP increases the sharing economy in the car industry by doing away with middlemen and offering a safe platform for trustless transactions. By reaching these goals, VOLR BP hopes to revolutionize the car ownership, leasing, and rental landscape, revolutionizing the way vehicles are transacted, and economic and environmental sustainability.

5   Proposed Protocol Architecture

The technology used by VOLR Blockchain is to create digital twins of automobiles and transform how vehicles are represented and managed on the blockchain by generating distinctive digital twins in the form of Non-Fungible Tokens (NFTs). This process begins at the manufacturer's end through their digital wallet, ensuring the creation of a secure and tamper-proof representation of the vehicle's information.

5.1   Digital Twin Creation

The Digital Twin Creation process is started by the maker, outfitted with a digital wallet integrated with the VOLR Blockchain. This digital wallet acts as a safe place to store, manage, and communicate with the NFTs that stand in for the vehicle.

5.2   Vehicle Identification Number (VIN)

The vehicle's manufacturer obtains its Vehicle Identification Number (VIN), a special number that sets it apart from other vehicles. The brand, model, manufacturing year, and serial number-along with other vital details-are all included in the vehicle identification number (VIN).

5.3   Digital Twin Minting

The manufacturer's digital wallet starts the minting procedure to produce a corresponding NFT, which serves as the vehicle's digital twin on the VOLR Blockchain, using the VIN as a reference. The metadata and attributes of the vehicle are encoded into the NFT during the minting process to guarantee its legitimacy.

5.4   Metadata and Attributes

The digital twin of the vehicle's NFT is connected to a wide range of metadata and attributes. The VIN, make, model, manufacturing year, color, mileage, maintenance history, and any other pertinent details deemed necessary by the manufacturer or according to industry standards are included in this data.

5.5   Blockchain Integration

The manufacturer's digital wallet communicates with the VOLR Blockchain after the NFT is created in order to safely keep the NFT that represents the digital twin. The digital twin of the car is guaranteed to be immutable and transparent thanks to the integration because it joins the decentralized ledger.

5.6   Transferability and Ownership

The VOLR Blockchain ecosystem allows for the transfer of the NFT, which stands for the digital twin of the vehicle, from the manufacturer's digital wallet to other stakeholders like dealers or customers. The blockchain keeps track of every transfer, making the ownership history transparent and auditable. The Digital Twin Creation method offers a trustworthy and traceable representation of the vehicle's information by minting NFTs using the vehicle VIN and safely storing them on the VOLR Blockchain. This facilitates effective vehicle ownership, leasing, and rental operations by allowing numerous stakeholders to access accurate and unchangeable records of the vehicle's history. It also increases transparency and confidence, as depicted in Figs. 2.

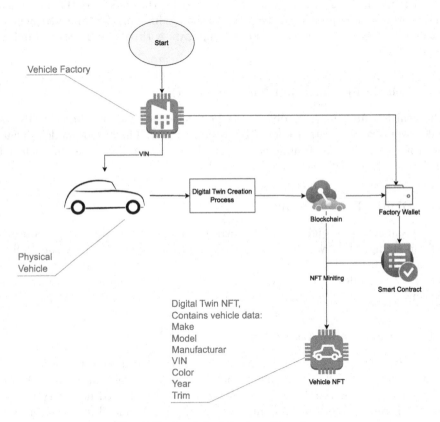

Fig. 2. Protocol Architecture Overview.

6   Protocol Operation

By utilizing smart contracts, which represent the terms and conditions of these transactions, the VOLR Blockchain protocol accelerates the processes for buying, leasing, and renting vehicles. These automated, secure exchanges between parties made possible by smart contracts guarantee openness, effectiveness, and conformity to predetermined terms. When payments are not made on time, the related NFT can be revoked by the smart contract, adding another layer of enforcement like shown in Fig. 3

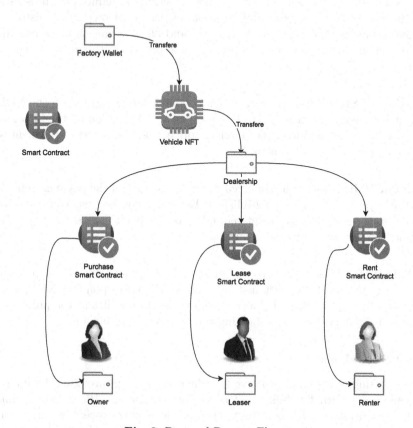

Fig. 3. Protocol Process Flow.

6.1 Vehicle Purchase

Vehicle purchase is a significant transaction that involves the transfer of ownership from a seller to a buyer. With the advent of blockchain technology, the vehicle purchase process can be revolutionized to ensure transparency, security, and efficiency. Through the use of smart contracts and Non-Fungible Tokens (NFTs), blockchain enables a streamlined and automated approach to vehicle purchase. Smart contracts embody the terms and conditions of the purchase agreement, including payment schedules, price, and delivery details. These contracts are executed on the blockchain, providing an immutable and auditable record of the transaction. NFTs represent the digital twins of vehicles, uniquely identifying each vehicle and recording its ownership status. As the buyer fulfills their payment obligations according to the smart contract, the associated NFT is transferred to their digital wallet, signifying the successful completion of the purchase and the transfer of ownership. This blockchain-based vehicle purchase process enhances trust, eliminates fraudulent activities, reduces administrative burden, and provides a clear and transparent record of ownership history. It empowers buyers and sellers with a secure and efficient means of transacting, making vehicle purchase a seamless and reliable process in the modern automotive industry.

Creation of Smart Contracts. A smart contract is generated on the VOLR Blockchain when a buyer wants to buy a car. The information on the buyer and seller, the vehicle's features, the purchase price, and the terms of payment are all included in this smart contract.

Payment Validation. The smart contract keeps track of the payment schedule that the buyer and seller have established. The smart contract will cause specified actions, such as sending payment reminders or applying fines if the buyer fails to make the necessary payments on time.

NFT Transfer. When the buyer completes the transaction in accordance with the terms, the smart contract instantly moves the corresponding NFT, which represents the digital twin of the car, from the seller's wallet to the purchaser's wallet to the buyer's wallet, indicating the transfer of ownership.

6.2   Vehicle Lease

Vehicle leasing offers an alternative to vehicle ownership, providing individuals and businesses with flexibility and cost-effective options. Blockchain technology brings transformative benefits to the vehicle leasing process by introducing transparency, security, and efficiency. Through the use of smart contracts and Non-Fungible Tokens (NFTs), the leasing process becomes streamlined and automated. Smart contracts embody the lease terms, including duration, monthly payments, mileage restrictions, and additional obligations. These contracts are executed on the blockchain, creating a transparent and immutable record of the agreement. NFTs represent the digital twins of leased vehicles, allowing for easy tracking and verification of the vehicle's usage and condition. The smart contract monitors the lessee's payments, ensuring compliance with the agreed terms. In the event of missed payments, the smart contract may initiate penalties or reminders. At the end of the lease term, the vehicle is returned, and the NFT is transferred back to the lessor's digital wallet, concluding the lease agreement. This blockchain-based vehicle leasing process enhances trust, provides auditable transaction history, and streamlines administrative tasks. It offers a secure and efficient solution, enabling seamless and reliable vehicle leasing experiences for both lessors and lessees in the modern automotive landscape.

Smart Contract Creation. In a scenario involving car leasing, the lessor and lessee create a smart contract on the VOLR Blockchain. The lease's tenure, monthly payment amount, mileage limitations, and any other duties are all described in the contract's terms and conditions. The smart contract keeps track of the lessee's recurring monthly lease payments. The smart contract may impose fines, send notifications, or carry out other specified actions if the lessee fails to make the payments on time.

Payment Monitoring. The smart contract monitors the lessee's monthly lease payments. If the lessee fails to make the payments on time, the smart contract may trigger penalties, send reminders, or initiate actions based on the agreed-upon terms.

NFT and Usage Tracking. The digital counterpart of the vehicle's NFT stays in the lessor's wallet for the duration of the lease. The smart contract keeps track of the vehicle's usage, including miles and maintenance, to ensure adherence to the agreed-upon conditions.

Lease Termination. The smart contract automatically ends the lease when the agreed-upon term expires. The car can be returned by the lessee, and the NFT ownership can be returned to the lessor's account if all conditions have been satisfied.

6.3   Vehicle Rental

Vehicle rental differed from vehicle leasing in the term, rentals normally are shorter term leases. The main advantage of using blockchain is the speed of settlement. Smart contracts allow finality in a matter of minutes without the need for excessive documentation.

Smart Contract Creation. When a vehicle is rented out, a smart contract is created on the VOLR Blockchain, detailing the terms and conditions of the rental agreement. This includes the rental duration, rental fee, payment schedule, and any penalties for late returns or damages.

Payment Verification. The smart contract verifies the renter's payment schedule. If the renter fails to make the required payments on time, the smart contract can impose penalties, trigger reminders, or initiate actions based on the agreed-upon terms.

NFT Transfer and Usage Tracking. The NFT representing the vehicle's digital twin remains with the rental service provider until the rental period ends. The smart contract tracks the vehicle's usage, ensuring compliance with rental terms, and facilitates real-time tracking of the vehicle's location and condition.

Rental Conclusion. When the rental period concludes, the smart contract finalizes the agreement. If all obligations have been met, the renter returns the vehicle, and the NFT ownership is transferred back to the rental service provider's wallet. By utilizing smart contracts, the VOLR Blockchain protocol automates and enforces the terms and conditions of vehicle purchase, lease, and rental transactions. The inclusion of NFTs as digital twins ensures transparent ownership records, while the smart contract's ability to revoke the NFT in case of nonpayment adds an additional layer of security and enforcement to these transactions.

7 Conclusion

The Vehicle Ownership, Leasing, and Rental Blockchain Protocol (VOLR BP) presented in this paper demonstrates the potential of blockchain technology and Non-Fungible Tokens (NFTs) in revolutionizing the automotive industry. By addressing the challenges associated with vehicle ownership, leasing, and rental, VOLR BP offers a robust and innovative solution that enhances transparency, trust, and operational efficiency. Protocol offers significant potential to revolutionize the automotive industry by introducing greater transparency, security, and efficiency in vehicle ownership, leasing, and rental processes. By leveraging the power of blockchain technology, this protocol addresses several key challenges and provides numerous benefits to all stakeholders involved. The benefits of VOLR BP extend beyond individual transactions and extend to the broader automotive ecosystem. The protocol presents opportunities for peer-to-peer vehicle sharing, promoting collaborative consumption, and expanding the sharing economy within the industry. By eliminating intermediaries, reducing costs, and increasing efficiency, VOLR BP has the potential to reshape the automotive landscape and unlock new possibilities for individuals, businesses, and emerging mobility services. However, it is important to note that the widespread adoption of the Blockchain Vehicle Ownership, Leasing, and Rental Protocol faces a few challenges. Firstly, regulatory frameworks and legal standards need to adapt to accommodate the decentralized nature of blockchain-based transactions. Governments and authorities must establish guidelines to ensure compliance, consumer protection, and liability in this new paradigm. In conclusion, the Blockchain Vehicle Ownership, Leasing, and Rental Protocol hold immense promise for transforming the way we own, lease, and rent vehicles. By leveraging the decentralized and transparent nature of blockchain technology, this protocol can provide secure and efficient solutions, foster trust among participants, and enable a more inclusive and sustainable automotive industry. However, addressing regulatory challenges, ensuring scalability, and promoting interoperability will be crucial for its widespread adoption and long-term success.

Acknowledgment. The authors would like to acknowledge AlphaFin, WebDBTech, Health Reasoning, Malak ElMessiry, Azza Shehata, Natalia Smirnova, and Open AI for their support.

References

1. Alippi, C., Bogdanovic, A., Roveri, M.: Big data analytics for secure industrial internet of things-driven automotive systems. IEEE Trans. Industr. Inf. **13**(4), 1995–2004 (2017)

2. ElMessiry, M., ElMessiry, A.: Blockchain framework for textile supply chain management. In: Chen, S., Wang, H., Zhang, L.-J. (eds.) ICBC 2018. LNCS, vol. 10974, pp. 213–227. Springer, Cham (2018). https://doi.org/10.1007/978-3-319-94478-4_15

3. ElMessiry, M., ElMessiry, A., ElMessiry, M.: Dual token blockchain economy framework. In: Joshi, J., Nepal, S., Zhang, Q., Zhang, L.-J. (eds.) ICBC 2019. LNCS, vol. 11521, pp. 157–170. Springer, Cham (2019). https://doi.org/10.1007/978-3-030-23404-1_11

4. Elmessiry, A., Bridgesmith, L.: A call for an artificial intelligence constitution. Available at SSRN 4120592 (2022)

5. Treiblmaier, H.: Combining blockchain technology and the physical internet to achieve triple bottom line sustainability: a comprehensive research agenda for modern logistics and supply chain management. Logistics **3**(1), 10 (2019). https://doi.org/10.3390/logistics3010010

6. Alcarria, R., Robles, T., Sanchez, L.: Blockchain for secure electric vehicle charging management. In: Proceedings of the 20th Conference on Innovation in Clouds, Internet and Networks and Workshops, pp. 351–356. IEEE (2017)

7. Ding, M., Dong, Z.Y., Xu, X.: A blockchain-based vehicle lifecycle data sharing system. IEEE Access **7**, 64382–64393 (2019)

8. Liu, Q., Li, C., Jin, X.: Blockchain-based trusted vehicle positioning in vanets. IEEE Trans. Veh. Technol. **68**(3), 2089–2101 (2019)

9. Martin, S., Martin-Meizoso, M., Burguillo-Rial, J.C.: Blockchain-based traceability systems in the automotive industry: a review of applications, challenges, and future opportunities. Automotive Innovation (2021)

10. Zheng, Z., Xie, S., Dai, H.N., Chen, X., Wang, H.: Blockchain challenges and opportunities: A survey. Int. J. Web Grid Serv. **14**(4), 352–375 (2018)

11. IBM Institute for Business Value: Distributed ledger technology: Leveraging blockchain for automotive. Technical report (2017)

12. Accenture: Blockchain technology in the automotive industry. Technical report (2018)

13. Deloitte: Blockchain in the automotive industry. Technical report (2018)

14. Wang, H., Wang, Y., Zeadally, S., Liu, R.: Blockchain-enabled electric vehicles in smart grids: a comprehensive review. IEEE Trans. Intell. Transp. Syst. **20**(6), 2224–2238 (2019)

15. Foroughi, F., Ghezavati, V., Souilah, W.: Blockchain technology for enhancing supply chain resilience in the automotive industry. Transp. Res. Part E (2021)

16. Kang, J.M., Kim, J.S., Kim, J.K.: A secure and efficient vehicle data sharing scheme using blockchain in vanets. IEEE Trans. Industr. Inf. **14**(6), 2671–2680 (2018)

17. PwC: Blockchain in the automotive sector. Technical report (2019)

18. Zyskind, G., Nathan, O., Pentland, A.: Decentralizing privacy: using blockchain to protect personal data. In: 2015 IEEE Security and Privacy Workshops, pp. 180–184. IEEE (2015)

19. Xu, X., Chen, H., Liu, X., Xu, Y.: A blockchain-based framework for vehicle lifecycle data management. IEEE Trans. Industr. Inf. **14**(4), 1433–1442 (2018)

20. Reddy M, K.M., Venkatesh, V., Prasad, K.S.: Blockchain-based vehicle history and ownership management system. Int. J. Sci. Eng. Res. (2018)
21. Wang, J., Zhang, H.: Blockchain for intelligent transportation systems: Opportunities and challenges. J. Adv. Transp. (2020)
22. Lavrut, T.: Blockchain technology: possibilities for the automotive industry. In: SAE Technical Paper (2019)

Author Index

© The Editor(s) (if applicable) and The Author(s), under exclusive license
to Springer Nature Switzerland AG 2023
Q. Wang et al. (Eds.): ICBC 2023, LNCS 14206, p. 147, 2023.
https://doi.org/10.1007/978-3-031-44920-8

Printed in the United States
by Baker & Taylor Publisher Services